Searching for Science Policy

Jonathan B. Imber
editor

Searching for Science Policy

Routledge
Taylor & Francis Group
LONDON AND NEW YORK

First published 2002 by Transaction Publishers

Published 2017 by Routledge
2 Park Square, Milton Park, Abingdon, Oxon OX14 4RN
711 Third Avenue, New York, NY 10017, USA

First issued in paperback 2017

Routledge is an imprint of the Taylor & Francis Group, an informa business

Copyright © 2002 by Taylor & Francis.

All rights reserved. No part of this book may be reprinted or reproduced or utilised in any form or by any electronic, mechanical, or other means, now known or hereafter invented, including photocopying and recording, or in any information storage or retrieval system, without permission in writing from the publishers.

Notice:
Product or corporate names may be trademarks or registered trademarks, and are used only for identification and explanation without intent to infringe.

Library of Congress Catalog Number: 2002028928

Library of Congress Cataloging-in-Publication Data

Searching for science policy / Jonathan B. Imber, editor.
    p. cm.
    "The chapters of this volume origniated in a conference entitled 'The use and misuses of science in public discourse' held at Boston University on April 1 and 2, 2000"—Introd.
    Includes bibliographical references and index.
    ISBN 0-7658-0163-9 (alk. paper)
    1. Policy sciences—Congresses. 2. Science and state—Congresses. 3. Social policy—Congresses. I. Imber, Jonathan B., 1952-

H97 .S4 2002
320'.6—dc21

2002028928

ISBN 13: 978-1-138-51442-3 (pbk)
ISBN 13: 978-0-7658-0163-0 (hbk)

Contents

Introduction: What are the Uses and Misuses of Science?
    Jonathan B. Imber   vii

Part 1: Policy Uses and Misuses of Science

1. How to Make Millions: Promoting Bad Statistics
    Joel Best   3
2. Exposing Junk Science.com: The Case of the MIT "Study" on the Status of Women
    Judith Kleinfeld   15
3. American Distortion of Dutch Drug Statistics
    Robert J. MacCoun   31
4. Science in *A Civil Action*
    Allan Mazur   39

Part 2: Searching for Science Policy

5. The Use and Abuse of Science in Drug Abuse Control Policy
    Mark A. R. Kleiman   51
6. Social Science Findings and the "Family Wars"
    Norval Glenn   67
7. Environmental Cancer
    Stanley Rothman and S. Robert Lichter   83
8. Judicial Fictions: The Supreme Court's Quest for Good Science
    Sheila Jasanoff   97

Contributors   117
Name Index   119

Introduction: What are the Uses and Misuses of Science?

Jonathan B. Imber

The chapters in this volume originated in a conference entitled "The Uses and Misuses of Science in Public Discourse" held at Boston University on April 1 and 2, 2000, under the auspices of the Institute for the Study of Economic Culture, in collaboration with *Society*, and with the generous support of the Lynde and Harry Bradley Foundation. I am personally grateful to Peter Berger for his vision of constructive social science and for his support in making the conference an important occasion to reflect on the broader meanings of science in society. Scientific research and the findings of such research ought to provide an important base line to the formulation of public policy in all sectors of society. Government, business, and universities are producers, consumers, and often arbiters of scientific research and findings. In assessing the uses and misuses of science, particularly in public discourse, the chapters contained here offer innovative ways of thinking about how the rhetoric and practice of science operate in various institutional contexts.

The communication to the larger public of what scientists do and know is a problem inherent to all democratic societies. It should not be seen as a kind of problem which is resolved by either limiting communication or delimiting the democratic process. Nevertheless, communicating complicated scientific findings to a jury or to an anxious public is fraught with difficulties that these essays seek to describe and clarify. Scientific truth cannot be put to a vote, even though it has been one prerogative of democratic societies to determine what kind of scientific research is funded, based upon the expectations of scientists themselves. It is often a complex and complicated matter.

The late Edward Shils, who taught sociology at the University of Chicago for forty years, wrote in 1987, "Scientists have become part of the political public in a way in which they have never been before." In a personal account of the role that scientists played in the aftermath of the creation of the atomic bomb, he noted that the Cold War created a climate in which scientists, who recognized the fundamental truths about nature which they were unlocking, were viewed as unreliable. Shils explained that "no one country could prevent another country from rediscovering the fundamental truths already discovered by other scientists" and that the scientists themselves believed this very much. The unreliability of scientists in the age of Cold War secrecy was thus less about their political affiliations and more about what the internet has lately taught us again: lies may abound and be difficult to correct, but fundamental truths are also difficult to keep secret.

Yet as Shils presciently observed, "The alarm about environmental damage resulting from the negligent disposal of chemical waste, the contention about the disposal of nuclear waste, the new sensitivity to dangers from pharmaceutical substances, anxiety about the potentialities of molecular biology and the technology based on it, and a deep fear of the destruction of human life by nuclear warfare have generated a tendency toward an 'anti-science' attitude in the intellectual classes and more widely." Our skepticism about science is less about the concealment of its fundamental truths among nations and much more about the determination of its uses within and beyond them. There are reasons to be wary of too much of an anti-science attitude, especially in universities. I am not referring to the fiascoes about postmodernists who believe that gravity is a social construction but rather about how citizenship in democratic societies is affected, and I believe deeply affected, by the rush to judgment that is too often cloaked in scientific claims.

Policy Uses and Misuses of Science

In part 1, four chapters are devoted to the question of the ways in which scientific claims themselves are inevitably mediated by their uses in various institutional spheres. Joel Best shows how the motivations to use inaccurate and misleading numbers stems directly from the ideological and institutional interests of those using them. Numbers are a substitute for authority in situations where ideological requirements demand that any principled disagreements about how to address a problem must be subordinated to the *urgency* of the problem itself. In this way, the most grotesque examples of such claims, for example, the stranger abduction of enormous numbers of children a year, prey upon the anxieties of parents with young children, guaranteeing that these anxieties will help garner attention for those peddling such nonsense. Nothing could be simpler and more publicly dynamic than the use of bad statistics for allegedly noble goals. The enduring problem is that the *real* frequency of problems, however defined, are not communicated. Instead, the *unreal* frequency of problems prompts attention and drives resources in directions that allow for little verification of or debate about the facts available.

Verification is one of the central problems of scientific advance, and it is not surprising that even among scientists themselves, the grounds for verification are often in dispute. As Judith Kleinfeld explains, the efforts to set policy among university faculty are driven by extra-scientific factors, and this is, presumably, how it should and inevitably must be. Yet precisely under the cloak of scientific justification, the changes in policy adopted by MIT with respect to its women scientists were defended as legitimate and necessary. Kleinfeld explains that this could not possibly be the case if fact-finding is the basis to policy recommendation because MIT officials refused to allow public scrutiny of the evidence cited to justify its actions. My impression is that Kleinfeld is not objecting in any way to MIT's internal decisions about its prerogative to reward its faculty as it sees fit, but she finds the public justifications for doing so, based on alleged scientific evidence, not only disconcerting but undermining of the core values of the university itself. Verification is a principle of scientific integrity, and by claiming to use the equivalent of scientific findings for its policy decisions, one of the great schools of science diminished its *raison d'être*, allowing ideological justification to trump objective scrutiny and evaluation.

Kleinfeld exposes this junk science in MIT's public formulation of internal policy. The Internet has become a source of rapid communication among otherwise separate sources of information. The second and perhaps more surprising part of her account comes in how challenges to MIT's public relations were mounted by the communication, among various individuals unknown to one another, about the claims of the unreleased study. It is difficult to embarrass an institution, and the effect is ephemeral in any case. After Kleinfeld's effort, MIT is unlikely to repeat itself, at least so publicly, in this way. But the question remains why reputable scientists, however disgruntled, would resort to the tactics described to acquire more resources. Part of the answer must be the narcissism of small differences, that is, part of the answer comes with appraising the personal scale in which such disputes are engaged. The competition is intense, and the grudges unsurprising. The future is nonetheless bright given where such internal disagreements occur. But MIT has a responsibility to all those lesser places parroting such procedures for their own grievances. This represents a profound failure in the ranks of elite institutions. They do not recognize how much they are noticed, and it is no wonder that a mushy-feminist-Marxist hangover has lasted so long in such places, leading to a loss of belief that the funding of science must finally be about what gets accomplished rather than by whom it gets accomplished. Any pretense of greatness is assigned to institutional policy rather than to individual activity, something that administrators prefer in this era of advanced bureaucratization of scientific work.

Robert J. MacCoun offers what Joel Best might describe as a natural history of the misuse of drug statistics. In this case, a journalist for the Associated Press gave notice to an article by MacCoun and Peter Reuter, constructing a false comparison between the use of marijuana in the United States and the Netherlands, thus profoundly distorting both what was being compared as well as what policy implications could be drawn from the data reported. MacCoun learned quickly what Best means by such distortions taking on a life of their own.

What MacCoun adds to our understanding of these distortions, beyond the sociological processes of their creation, is a preliminary elaboration of the psychological or cognitive implications of appropriating scientific data for public policy pronouncements. MacCoun remarks on the ways that hot and cold forms of cognition lend themselves to different types of distortion in the uses of data. At the same time, he acknowledges the all-too-human features of passionate debate. In some respects, American drug policy carries forward those processes of moralization that have long marked the American response to deviant behavior. At the same time, MacCoun's important argument is that if the data are taken seriously, a more nuanced and less rushed judgment about what may or may not work here and there will eventually emerge, even in the corridors of power. Journalists need to learn more about social statistics and how to communicate what may very often appear to be, at the level of policy, contradictory findings about what is and is not working. This is a difficult task under any circumstance, but it is also among the highest ethical ambitions of social science, which the waves of ideological, moralizing, and self-interested constituencies always threaten to overwhelm and undermine. Social science in an age of multiple fanaticisms has good cause to be what might be called constructively paranoid. Aware of the fragile nature of their own insights, social scientists must be all the more vigilant in drawing a bright line between activism and analysis.

One test of the broad importance of scientific understanding in modern societies is the role that scientific evidence has come to play in the law. Allan Mazur neatly and concisely lays out the pitfalls of the double-reliance on scientific evidence, first in terms of its intrinsic quality and then in terms of its appropriation and interpretation by judges and juries charged with rendering verdicts. In the majority of cases, the principal issue at hand is the determination of harm to plaintiffs. Historically, such determinations were based on the reports of witnesses and less on forensic evidence. The development of scientific method in the collection, evaluation, and presentation of evidence has long influenced the ways in which cases are argued —the legal case incorporates a rhetoric of persuasion that scientific debate does not, at least not as an end in itself. Mazur, in the open spirit of social-scientific inquiry, calls for careful accounting of whether judges and juries are able to perform their functions more or less effectively depending upon how expert witnesses providing scientific accounts are permitted to be used in courts.

Searching for Science Policy

Part 2 consists of four contributions that extend the discussion of the role of science to specific ideas about improving the formulation of drug policy, family policy, environmental policy and health, and judicial policy and its uses of science. In his brief illustrations of four policy questions about alcohol taxation, prison sentences for cocaine dealers, methadone maintenance policy, and anti-drug education, Mark Kleiman delineates the constructive aims of science as an independent activity in the search for truth over and regularly against the constructive aims of social policy deliberations in the search for effective measures of social control. Those in pursuit of research and program resources need to outline more clearly their goals, and they must be willing to bear greater public scrutiny of the various costs and benefits. It would help if the politics of science could be made more explicit for the purposes of illuminating the inherent conflict of interests that arise between a search for truth and a search for order. Kleiman knows well the dangers of retreating from scientific argument and evaluation, and at the same time, he appreciates how the failure of American drug policy provides the opportunity to lay out a new agenda for determining what does and does not work in this contentious realm of policy formation.

Norval Glenn, in his review of the social science research on the family, concludes, "The ultimate purpose of discussing constructive and inappropriate uses of social science finding is of course to try to contribute to an increase of the ratio of the former to the latter." Glenn recognizes that any vigilance about the ways in which social-scientific findings are reported to the public is not easily formulated in terms of policy; it involves collaboration among professional associations, the media, and researchers themselves. Unfortunately, candor about the *limitations* of such findings is less ethically imperative than the impulse to report *something*, thus making many of the disputes about what we know about the family susceptible to political and ideological polarization.

The extent to which professional associations lend their authority (and credibility) to something less than disinterest in the research findings of their membership, creates the conditions for public distrust of social science generally. This applies equally to the creation of textbooks, which are supposed to convey something more than the ideological agendas of researchers. But, Glenn, advises, "Social scientists cannot remain aloof from ideological debates, and they should not try to do so, but they should, insofar as possible, make sure that their most important 'significant others' are those who value objectivity and consider changing one's mind on a controversial issue to be a badge of honor rather than an occasion for embarrassment." Such a possibility requires decisive leadership, role models, and instructive examples. Norval Glenn's distinguished research career embodies all three.

Stanley Rothman and S. Robert Lichter provide a synopsis of their larger research into the ways in which communication of scientific findings shapes the public's understanding of environmental risks. Their meticulous empirical description of the ways in which risks about environmental cancer are reported in mainstream media reveals the deeper cultural biases that always tend to reinforce the *incidence* of an alleged harm over and against its relative frequency among a broad range of such harms. Their research provides an important baseline for understanding the dynamic nature of social movements (e.g., environmental organizations) in relation to public perceptions of risk and harm. The articulation of such a dynamic ought to be considered a scientific advance, because it underlies the improvement of the relations among a complex set of social groups, including journalists, scientists, and public advocacy groups, thus diminishing confusion in the public mind about their specific roles. Skepticism is a virtue in scientific discourse, and it now extends beyond the specific processes of scientific investigation itself to the public assertions of many groups, asserting scientific authority for their various claims. And so it is with some sense of optimism that Rothman and Lichter acknowledge that the earlier stages of exaggerated concern about environmental cancer have matured into a more constructive and informative collaboration among all concerned parties.

Finally, Sheila Jasanoff returns the discussion of the practical implications of science in society by taking up again the concerns that Allan Mazur addresses at the end of part 1 of this volume. Jasanoff looks closely at the different rhythms and temperaments of science in its normal practices and in the more contentious sphere of litigation – the former may not easily reach ultimate resolutions about causation, for example, though litigation requires some form of outcome, whether acquittal, liability, or settlement somewhere in between. Scientific proof and legal proof cannot be reduced one to the other. On the contrary, she makes clear how the relative credibility of scientific evidence most likely improves over time, precisely as that evidence accrues in the accumulated weight of scrutiny, replication, and public dissemination. She worries nevertheless that even at its highest ranks, the judiciary appears unaccountable to the rough and tumble of scientific debate, cultivating in effect its own private views about science that influence the ways in which judges then appropriate and use scientific evidence at trial.

It appears that part of the problem that Jasanoff and other contributors have identified very well is the fact that science is both the basis of much of modern understanding as well as the all-important agent of change in that understanding. Uncertainty cannot be any longer only privately existential. It is tied instead to what science can predict, rather more effectively than ever before, about the fate of individuals and groups over time. Jasanoff quite perceptively observes, following the sociologist Ulrich Beck, that the conditions for achieving justice in societies, whose core values rest upon a faith in science, may never (as a result of the nature of scientific truth) achieve final establishment of causation about many things that injure and shorten lives. A rational acceptance of uncertainty requires a different kind of approach to litigation, something that may, in fact, be evermore important to achieve, given the wildly disparate outcomes of litigation. Indeed, something of the reflective authority of judges becomes all the more important.

The well-informed citizen is no longer a moral ideal but rather a social imperative in a time when scientists find themselves subject to more public scrutiny than ever before. This scrutiny is a good thing because it represents a belief in the public's ability to face up to uncertainty about both individual and collective futures. We need more efforts such as those contained in this volume to clarify the grounds and the circumstances of effective uses of science in public discourse. Scientific truth is not in the eye of the beholder. Just as capitalism was once a pejorative naming by its opponents, so globalization in recent years has been subject to relentless criticisms. What are concealed in such criticisms are two features that make such criticisms possible: science and reason. The historical substitute for globalization, in the final analysis, is not capitalism, but rather science. Scrutiny of science, while appreciating the grounds on which such scrutiny is possible, is the bargain we make with reason in a world always tending to substitute ideology and narcissism in its place. As these essays compellingly illustrate, enlightenment is, and always has been, and will remain, difficult work.

Part 1

Policy Uses and Misuses of Science

1

How to Make Millions: Promoting Bad Statistics

Joel Best

In contemporary society, social problems must compete for attention.[1] To the degree that one problem gains media coverage, moves to the top of politicians' agendas, or becomes the subject of public concern, others will be neglected. Advocates find it necessary to make compelling cases for the importance of particular social problems. They choose persuasive wording and point to disturbing examples, and they usually bolster their case with dramatic statistics.

Statistics have a fetish-like power in contemporary discussions about social problems. We pride ourselves on rational policymaking, and our rationality is guided by expertise and evidence. Statistics become central to the process: numbers evoke science and precision; they seem to be nodules of truth, facts that distill the simple essence of apparently complex social processes. In a culture that treats facts and opinions as dichotomous terms, numbers signify truth—what we call "hard facts." In virtually every social problems debate, statistics trump "mere opinion."

Yet social problems statistics often involve dubious data. While critics occasionally call some number into question, it generally is not necessary for a statistic to be accurate—or even plausible—in order to achieve widespread acceptance. Advocates seeking to promote social problems often worry more about the processes by which policy makers, the press, and the public come to focus on particular problems, than about the quality of their figures. This paper seeks to identify some principles that govern this process. They are, if you will, guidelines for creating and disseminating dubious social problems statistics.

Although we talk about facts as though they exist independent of people, patiently awaiting our discovery, people have to produce—or construct—all that we know. Every social statistic reflects the choices that go into producing it. The key choices involve definition and methodology: whenever we count something, we must first define what it is we hope to count, and then choose the methods by which we will go about counting. Every student of sociological research methods learns that these are consequential choices that shape every social statistic, but that basic lesson is often forgotten when numbers are introduced into policy debates.

In general, the press regards statistics as facts, little bits of truth. The human choices that lie behind every number are forgotten; the very presentation of a number gives a claim credibility. In this sense, statistics are fetishes. This suggests the first rule for contemporary policy debates:

1. Any number is better than no number

By this generous standard, a number need not bear close inspection, or even be remotely plausible. To choose an example first brought to light by Christina Hoff Sommers (1994), a number of recent books, both popular and scholarly, have repeated the garbled claim that anorexia kills 150,000 women annually. (The figure seems to have originated from an estimate for the total number of women who are anorexic; only about seventy die each year from the disease [Lawson 1885].) It should have been obvious that something was wrong with this figure. Anorexia typically affects *young* women. Each year, roughly 8,500 females aged fifteen to twenty-four die from all causes; another 47,000 women aged twenty-five to forty-four also die (U.S. Bureau of the Census 1997: 96). What are the chances, then, that there could be 150,000 deaths from anorexia each year? But, of course, most of us have no idea how many young women die each year—("It must be a lot. . . "). When we hear that anorexia kills 150,000 young women per year, we assume that whoever cites the number must know that it is true. It is, after all, a number and therefore presumably factual.

Oftentimes, social problems statistics exist in splendid isolation. When there is only one number, that number has the weight of authority. It is accepted and repeated. People treat the statistic as authoritative because, well, because it's a statistic. Often, these lone numbers come from activists seeking to draw attention to neglected social phenomena. One symptom of societal neglect is that no one has bothered to do much research or compile careful records; there often are no official statistics or other sources for more accurate numbers. When reporters cover the story, they want to report facts. When activists have the only available figures, their numbers look like facts, so, in the absence of other numbers, the media simply report the activists' statistics.

Once a number appears in one news report, that story becomes a potential source for everyone seeking information about the social problem; officials, experts, activists, and other reporters routinely repeat figures that appear in press reports.

2. Numbers take on lives of their own

David F. Luckenbill refers to this as "number laundering." A statistic's origin—perhaps simply as someone's best guess—is soon forgotten, and through repetition, the figure comes to be treated as a straightforward fact—accurate and authoritative. The trail becomes muddy—people lose track of the estimate's original source, but they become confident that the number must be correct because it appears everywhere.

It barely matters if critics challenge a number, and expose it as erroneous. Once a number is in circulation, it can live on, regardless of how thoroughly it may have been discredited. Today's improved methods of information retrieval—electronic indexes, full-text databases, and the Internet—make it easier than ever to locate statistics. Anyone who locates a number can—and quite possibly will—repeat it. That annual toll of 150,000 anorexia deaths has been thoroughly debunked, yet the figure continues to appear in occasional newspaper stories. Electronic storage has given us astonishing, unprecedented access to information, but many people have terrible difficulty sorting through what's available and distinguishing good information from bad. Standards for comparing and evaluating claims seem to be wanting. This is particularly true for statistics, which are, after all, numbers and therefore factual, requiring no critical evaluation. Why not believe—and repeat—a number that everyone else uses?

Still, some numbers do have advantages. In particular, in describing social problems:

3. Big numbers are better than little numbers

Remember: social problems claims must compete for attention; there are many causes and a limited amount of space on the front page of the *New York Times*. Advocates must find ways to make their claims compelling; they favor melodrama—terrible villains, sympathetic, vulnerable victims, and big numbers. Big numbers suggest that there is a big problem, and big problems demand attention, concern, action—they must not be ignored.

Advocates seeking to attract attention to a social problem soon find themselves pressed for numbers. Press and policymakers demand facts—("You say it's a problem? Well, how big a problem is it?"). Activists believe in the problem's seriousness, and they often spend much of their time talking to others who share that belief. They know that the problem is much more serious, much more common than generally recognized—("The cases we know about are only the tip of the iceberg. . . "). So, when asked for figures, they offer their best estimates, educated guesses, guesstimates, ballpark figures, or stabs in the dark. Mitch Snyder, the most visible spokesperson for the homeless in the early 1980s, explained on ABC's *Nightline* how activists arrived at the figure of three million homeless: "Everybody demanded it. Everybody said we want a number . . . . We got on the phone, we made a lot of calls, we talked to a lot of people, and we said, 'Okay, here are some numbers.' They have no meaning, no value" (quoted in Jencks 1994: 2). Because activists sincerely believe that the new problem is big and important, and because they suspect that there is a very large dark figure of unreported or unrecorded cases, activists' estimates tend to be high, to err on the side of exaggeration.

This helps explain the tendency to estimate the scope of social problems in large, suspiciously round figures. There are, we are told, one million victims of elder abuse each year, two million missing children, three million homeless, 60 million functionally illiterate Americans; child pornography may be, depending on your source, a $1 billion—or $46 billion—industry, and so on. Often, these estimates are the only available numbers.

The mathematician John Allen Paulos (1988) argues that innumeracy—the mathematical counterpart to illiteracy—is widespread and consequential. He suggests that innumeracy particularly shapes the way we deal with large numbers. Most of us understand hundreds, even thousands, but soon the orders of magnitude blur into a single category: "It's a lot." Even the most implausible figures can gain widespread acceptance. When missing-children advocates charged that nearly two million children are missing each year, anyone might have done the basic math: there are about 60 million children under 18; if two million are missing, that would be one in thirty; that is, every year, the equivalent of one child in every American schoolroom would be missing—a 900-student school would have thirty children missing from its student body each year. To be sure, this statistic was debunked by the press in 1985—only four years after missing children became a highly publicized issue and the two-million estimate gained wide circulation (Griego and Kilzer 1985). And, of course, having been discredited, the number survives and can still be encountered on occasion.

It is remarkable how often contemporary discussions of social problems make no effort to define what is at issue. Often, we're given a dramatic, compelling example, perhaps a tortured, murdered child, then told that this terrible case is an example of a social problem—in this case, child abuse—and finally given a statistic: "There are more than three million reports of child abuse each year." The example, coupled with the problem's name, seems sufficient to make the definition self-evident.

However, definitions cannot always be avoided. This leads to our fourth principle:

4. Broad definitions are better than narrow definitions

Because broad definitions encompass more kinds of cases, they justify bigger numbers, and we have already noted the advantages of big numbers.

No definition is perfect; there are two principal ways definitions of social problems can be flawed. On the one hand, a definition might be too broad and encompass more than it ought to include. That is, broad definitions tend to identify what methodologists call false positives; they include some cases that arguably ought not to be included as part of the problem. On the other hand, a definition that is too narrow may exclude false negatives, cases that perhaps ought to be included as part of the problem.

In general, activists trying to promote a new social problem view false negatives as more troubling than false positives. Activists often feel frustrated trying to get people concerned about some social condition that has been ignored. The general failure to recognize and acknowledge that something is wrong is part of what the activists want to correct; therefore, they may be especially careful not to themselves make things worse by defining the problem too narrowly. A definition that is too narrow fails to recognize a problem's full extent; in doing so, it helps perpetuate the history of neglecting the problem. Some activists favor definitions broad enough to encompass every case that ought to be included; that is, they promote broad definitions in hopes of eliminating all false negatives.

However, broad definitions may invite criticism. They include cases that not everyone considers instances of social problems; that is, while they minimize false negatives, they do so at the cost of maximizing cases that critics may see as false positives. The rejoinder to this critique returns us to the idea of neglect and the harm it causes. Perhaps, advocates acknowledge, their definitions may seem to be too broad, to encompass cases that seem too trivial to be counted as instances of the social problem (Best 1999). But how can we make that judgement? Here, advocates are fond of pointing to terrible examples, to the victim whose one, brief, comparatively mild experience had terrible personal consequences; to the child who, having been exposed to a flasher, suffers a lifetime of devastating psychological consequences. Perhaps, advocates say, other victims with similar experiences suffer less—or at least seem to suffer less. But is it just to define a problem too narrowly to include everyone who suffers? Shouldn't our statistics measure the problem's full extent?

While social problems statistics often go unchallenged, critics occasionally suggest that some number is implausibly large, or that a definition is too broad:

5. The best way to defend a number is to attack its critics' motives

When activists have generated a statistic as part of a campaign to arouse concern about some social problem, there is a tendency for them to conflate the number with the cause. Therefore, anyone who questions a statistic can be suspected of being unsympathetic to the larger claims, indifferent to the victims' suffering, and so on. Ad hominem attack on the motives of individuals challenging numbers is a standard response to statistical confrontations. These attacks allow advocates to refuse to budge; making ad hominem arguments lets them imply that their opponents don't want to acknowledge the truth, that their statistics are derived from ideology, rather than methodology. If the advocates' campaign has been reasonably successful, they can argue that there is now widespread appreciation that this is a big, serious problem; after all, the advocates' number has been widely accepted and repeated—surely it must be correct. A fallback stance—useful in those rare cases where public scrutiny leaves one's own numbers completely discredited—is to treat the challenge as meaningless nitpicking. Perhaps our statistics were flawed, the advocates acknowledge, but the precise number hardly makes a difference—("After all, even one victim is too many.").

Similarly, criticizing definitions for being too broad can provoke angry reactions. For advocates, such critiques seem to deny victim's suffering, minimize the extent of the problem, and by extension endorse the status quo. If broader definitions reflect progress, more sensitive appreciation of the true scope of social problems, then calls for narrowing definitions are retrograde, insensitive refusals to confront society's flaws.

Of course, definitions must be operationalized if they are to lead to statistics. It is necessary to specify how the problem will be measured and the statistic produced. If there is to be a survey, who will be sampled? And how will the questions be worded? In what order will they be asked? How will the responses be coded? Most of what we call social scientific methodology involves choosing how to measure social phenomena. Every statistic depends upon these choices. Just as advocates' preference for large numbers leads them to favor broad definitions, the desirability of broad definitions shapes measurement choices:

6. Inclusive measures are better than exclusive measures

Most contemporary advocates have enough sociological sophistication to allude to the dark figure—that share of a social problem that goes unreported and unrecorded. Official statistics, they warn, inevitably underestimate the size of social problems. This undercounting helps justify advocates' generous estimates (recall all those references to "the tip of the iceberg"). Awareness of the dark figure also justifies measurement decisions that maximize researchers' prospects for discovering and counting as many cases as possible (cf. Smith 1994).

Consider the first federally sponsored National Incidence Studies of Missing, Abducted, Runaway, and Thrownaway Children (NISMART) (Finkelhor, Hotaling, and Sedlak 1990). This was an attempt to produce an accurate estimate for the numbers of missing children. To estimate family abductions (in which a family member kidnaps a child) researchers conducted a telephone survey of households. The researchers made a variety of inclusive measurement decisions: an abduction could involve moving a child as little as twenty feet; it could involve the child's complete cooperation; there was no minimum time that the abduction had to last; those involved may not have considered what happened an abduction; and there was no need that the child's whereabouts be unknown (in most family abductions identified by NISMART, the child was not with someone who had legal custody, but everyone knew where the child was). Using these methods of measurement, a non-custodial parent who took a child for an unauthorized visit, or who extended an authorized visit for an extra night, was counted as having committed a "family abduction"; if the same parent tried to conceal the taking or to prevent the custodial parent's contact with the child, the abduction was classified in the most serious ("policy-focal") category. The NISMART researchers concluded that there were 163,200 of these more serious family abductions each year, although evidence from states with the most thorough missing-children reporting systems suggests that only about 9,000 cases per year come to police attention. In other words, the researchers' inclusive measurement choices led to a remarkably high estimate. Media coverage of the family-abduction problem coupled this high figure with horrible examples—cases of abductions lasting years, involving long-term sexual abuse, ending in homicide, and so on. Although most of the episodes identified by NISMART's methods were relatively minor, the press implied that very serious cases were very common—("It's a big number!") (Best and Thibodeau 1997).

There is nothing atypical about the NISMART example. Advocacy research has become an important source of social problems statistics. Advocates hope research will produce large numbers, and tend to believe that broad definitions are justified. They deliberately adopt inclusive research measurements that promise to minimize false negatives and generate large numbers. These measurement decisions almost always occur outside public scrutiny and only rarely attract attention. When the media report numbers, percentages, and rates, they almost never explain the definitions and measurements used to produce those statistics.

While many statistics seem to stand alone, occasions do arise when there are competing numbers—contradictory statistical answers to what seems to be the same question. In general, the media tend to treat such competing numbers with a sort of even-handedness:

7. Competing numbers are equally good

Because the media tend to treat numbers as factual, and to ignore definitions and measurement choices, inconsistent numbers pose a problem. Clearly, both numbers cannot be correct. Where a methodologist might try to ask how different advocates arrived at different numbers (in hopes of showing that one figure is more accurate than another, or at least of understanding how the different numbers might be products of different methods), the press is more likely to account for any difference in terms of the competitors' conflicting ideologies or agendas.

Consider the case of the estimates for the crowd size at the 1995 Million Man March. The event's very name set a standard for its success: as the date for the March approached, its organizers insisted that it would attract a million people, while their critics predicted that the crowd would never reach that size. On the day of the march, the organizers announced success: there were, they said, 1.5 to 2 million people present. Alas, the National Park Service Park Police, charged by Congress with estimating the size of demonstrations on the Capitol Mall, calculated that the march drew only 400,000 people (still more than any previous civil rights demonstration). The Park Police knew the Mall's dimensions, took aerial photos, and multiplied the area covered by the crowd by a multiplier based on typical crowd densities. The organizers—like the organizers of many previous demonstrations on the Mall—insisted that the Park Police estimate was far too low. Enter a team of aerial photo analysts from Boston University who eventually calculated that the crowd numbered 837,000 plus or minus 25 percent (i.e., they suggested there might have been a million people in the crowd).

The press covered these competing estimates in standard he said-she said style. Few reporters bothered to ask why the two estimates were different. (The answer was simple: the BU researchers used a different multiplier. Where the Park Police estimated that there was one demonstrator per 3.6 square feet [actually a fairly densely-packed crowd], the BU researchers calculated that there was a person for every 1.8 square feet [the equivalent of being packed in a crowded elevator] [Daly and Harris 1995].) But rather than trying to compare or evaluate the processes by which people arrived at the different estimates, most press reports treated the numbers as equally valid, and implied that the explanation for the difference lay in the motives of those making the estimates. The March organizers (who wanted to argue that the demonstration had been successful) produced a high number; the Park Police (who—the March organizers insisted—were biased against the March) produced a low one, and the BU scientists (presumably impartial and authoritative) found something in between. The BU estimate quickly found favor in the media: it let the organizers save face (because the BU team conceded the crowd might have reached one million); it seemed to split the different between the high and low estimates; and it apparently came from experts. There was no effort to judge the competing methods and assumptions behind the different numbers, to ask whether it was likely that hundreds of thousands of men stood packed as close together as the BU researchers imagined for the hours the demonstration lasted.

This example, like those discussed earlier, reveals that public discussions of social statistics are remarkably unsophisticated. Social scientists advance their careers by using arcane inferential statistics to interpret data. The standard introductory undergraduate statistics textbook tends to zip through descriptive statistics on the way to inferential statistics. But it is descriptive statistics—simple counts, averages, percentages, rates, and the like—that play the key role is public discussions over social problems and social policy. And the level of those discussions is not terribly advanced. There is too little critical thinking about social statistics. People manufacture—and other people repeat—dubious figures. While this can involve deliberate attempts to deceive and manipulate, this need not be the case. Often, the people who create the numbers—who, as it were, make all those millions—believe in them. Neither the advocates who create statistics, nor the reporters who repeat them, nor the larger public questions the figures.

What Paulos calls innumeracy is partly to blame—many people aren't comfortable with basic ideas of numbers and calculations. But there is an even more fundamental issue: many of us do not appreciate that every number is a social construction, produced by particular people using particular methods. The naive—but widespread—tendency is to treat statistics as fetishes—almost magical nuggets of fact—rather than as someone's efforts to summarize, to simplify complexity. If we accept the statistic as fetish, then several of the guidelines I've outlined make perfect sense: any number is better than no number—because the number represents truth; numbers take on lives of their own—they live on because they are true, and their truth justifies their survival; the best way to defend a number is to attack its critics' motives—because anyone who questions a presumably true number must have dubious reasons for doing so; and, when we are confronted with competing numbers, those numbers are equally good—because, after all, they are somehow equivalent bits of truth. At the same time, the guidelines offer those who must produce numbers justifications for favoring big numbers, broad definitions, and inclusive methods. Again, this need not be cynical. Often, advocates are confident they know the truth, and they approach collecting statistics as a straightforward effort to generate the numbers needed to document what they, after all, know to be true.

Any effort to improve the quality of public discussion of social statistics needs to begin with the understanding that numbers are socially constructed. Statistics are not nuggets of objective fact that we discover; rather, they are people's creations. Every statistic reflects people's decisions to count, their choices of what to count and how to go about counting it, and so on. These choices inevitably shape the resulting numbers.

Public discussions of social statistics need to chart a middle path between naivete (the assumption that numbers are simply true) and cynicism (the suspicion that figures are outright lies told by people with bad motives). This middle path needs to be critical—to recognize that every statistic has to be created, to acknowledge that every statistic is imperfect, yet to appreciate that statistics still offer an essential way of summarizing complex information. Social scientists have a responsibility to promote this critical stance—in the public, within the press, and among advocates.

Note

1. Expanded discussions of many of the ideas in this essay may be found in Best (2001).

References

Best, Joel. 1999. *Random Violence: How We Talk about New Crimes and New Victims.* Berkeley: University of California Press.
_____. 2001. *Damned Lies and Statistics: Untangling Numbers from the Media, Politicians, and Activists.* Berkeley: University of California Press.
Best, Joel, and Tracy M. Thibodeau. 1997. "Measuring the Scope of Social Problems: Apparent Inconsistencies across Estimates of Family Abductions." *Justice Quarterly* 14: 719-37.
Daly, Christopher B., and Hamil R. Harris. 1995. "Boston U. Sets March at 837,000." *Washington Post* (October 28): C3.

Finkelhor, David., Gerald Hotaling, and Andrea Sedlak. 1990. *Missing, Abducted, Runaway, and Thrownaway Children in America*. Washington, DC: U.S. Office of Juvenile Justice and Delinquency Prevention.
Griego, Diana, and Louis Kilzer. 1985. "Truth about Missing Kids: Exaggerated Statistics Stir National Paranoia." *Denver Post* (May 12): 1A, 12A.
Jencks, Christopher. 1994. *The Homeless*. Cambridge, MA: Harvard University Press.
Lawson, Carol. 1985. "Doctors Cite Emetic Abuse." *American Anorexia/Bulimia Association Newsletter* (June): 1.
Paulos, John Allen. 1988. *Innumeracy: Mathematical Illiteracy and Its Consequences*. New York: Random House.
Smith, Michael D. 1994. "Enhancing the Quality of Survey Data on Violence against Women." *Gender and Society* 8: 109-27.
Sommers, Christina Hoff. 1994. *Who Stole Feminism?* New York: Simon & Schuster.
U.S. Bureau of the Census. 1997. *Statistical Abstract of the United States, 1997*, 117th ed. Washington, DC.

2

Exposing Junk Science.com: The Case of the MIT "Study" on the Status of Women

Judith Kleinfeld

The "MIT Study on the Status of Women" rocked the academic world. One of the most prestigious scientific institutions in the country, the Massachusetts Institute of Technology, publicly admitted to discriminating against its female faculty. The study was breathlessly and uncritically reported on the front page of the *New York Times* on March 23, 1999, and picked up by newspapers and academic publications across the nation. The MIT study quickly became a model for similar gender discrimination studies at institutions throughout the country and in Europe. Similar committees to investigate the treatment of female faculty were established, for example, at the University of Arizona, the University of Pennsylvania, the California Institute of Technology, and the Harvard Medical School.

According to MIT, their confession of gender discrimination was based on hard facts, such as findings of gender differences in the laboratory space allocated to male and female faculty. The dean of MIT's School of Science at the time, Robert J. Birgeneau, stated that the study was "data-driven," which is a "very MIT thing." Few bothered to read the study itself, published in a special edition of the *MIT Faculty Newsletter* in March 1999 and available on the MIT website.

The First Critique: "MIT Tarnishes Its Reputation with Junk Gender Science"

In a critique of the study, published by the Independent Women's Forum, I pointed out that that the MIT report actually presented no data whatsoever showing any gender differences in laboratory space or any other resource. Such data must be "confidential," said MIT, making the astonishing claim for a scientific institution that grouped data on such an innocuous matter as laboratory space cannot be made public but can be used to justify increased salary and other resources for certain female faculty.

In my critique, I also pointed out that MIT failed to follow the most elementary standards for the conduct of social research. MIT's means of investigating the complaint defied not only empirical science but also common sense. Nancy Hopkins, the professor who made the initial charges of gender discrimination, for example, was actually appointed head of the committee investigating her own complaints! Two-thirds of the committee's members were senior female faculty, the very women who would benefit if gender discrimination were found.

Not only did the "MIT Study on the Status of Women" provide no objective evidence of gender differences in salaries, space, the internal allocation of research funds, or any other resource. Even the female faculty's subjective feelings of gender bias were not evaluated according to elementary principles for coding data in the social sciences. A study of perceptions adhering to accepted scientific methods would include, at least in an appendix, the wording of the questions that were asked and a table showing the numbers of women expressing a range of attitudes.

A Second Critique Shows MIT Senior Women Are Lower than MIT Senior Men in Scientific Productivity

My critique only pointed out the lack of evidence for claims of gender discrimination by MIT. A second critique found dramatic differences in scientific productivity between MIT male and female faculty that could easily have justified any gender differences in prestige, pay, and perquisites. Two independent researchers, Patricia Hausman, a scholar in Washington, D.C., and James H. Steiger, a professor of psychology at the University of British Columbia, undertook a careful and rigorous comparison of male and female faculty based on publicly available information. In "Confession Without Guilt," they publish striking findings: The MIT senior female faculty who complained of gender discrimination were far less productive scientifically than their male counterparts.

Hausman and Steiger found two natural groups in the fifty-eight-member biology department, where the complaints of gender discrimination first arose: one made up of eleven senior professors who earned doctorates between 1970 and 1976 and the other made up of thirteen younger professors who earned their doctorates between 1988 and 1993. They compared the scientific productivity of male and female faculty in each group using such standard measures as number of publications, citations, and raising grant funding:

- Three of the six males but only one female published more than 100 papers between 1989 and 2000.

- Three of the six males had more than 10,000 citations—more than three times the number of citations as the most widely cited female.

- Three of the six males had brought in far more funding than all but one of the women. One male had brought in almost three times as much funding as the woman with the highest amount of funding.

If any differences in pay and perquisites did exist between male and female senior faculty, Hausman and Steiger point out, the explanation might well be the just result of the lower productivity of the senior female faculty in the biology department. A quite telling point is that the junior female faculty at MIT did *not* report gender discrimination: The Hausman and Steiger report found very little difference in scientific productivity between the junior male and female faculty in MIT's Biology Department.

This is precisely the type of scientific analysis that MIT itself should have done and did not. MIT did not refute either of the two critiques. It merely backed off in its claim that the report was "science" and now claimed that it was instead the result of an internal investigation. MIT proceeded blithely to convene a gender discrimination conference of prestigious institutions, including Harvard, Yale, and Stanford, which resulted in pious pledges to work toward gender equity.

Using the Internet to Publicize Critiques of Junk Science

Junk science is a difficult problem to expose when it comes to studies of feminist issues. Many reporters and their editors are sympathetic to stories of female victimization and rarely seek out contrary opinion. Even when reporters genuinely try to create balanced articles, they are hampered by the reluctance of scientists, particularly males, to speak out on the issue. The male scientists fear being branded as at best unsympathetic to the cause of the advancement of women in science and at worst as bigots, caught in paradigms of male domination. The consequences to their careers and reputations can be grave. Those who champion the cause of women, on the other hand, are rewarded, whatever the facts may be. MIT's Robert J. Birgeneau is a prime example. Partly as a result of his backing of the MIT senior women's grievances, he was awarded the presidency of the University of Toronto. While he later claimed he was misquoted, the *Toronto Star* said that he warned administrators who didn't share his view on diversity that they "may as well step down."

But the Internet has changed the nature of the game. For those who are willing to speak out on politically correct issues, the Internet has made it possible to bypass the media elite and make their arguments known. Using my own critique of the MIT study as a case example, "MIT Tarnishes Its Reputation with Junk Gender Science," I show how the Internet:

1. Ignited a national controversy on the scientific validity of the MIT Report that would otherwise have fizzled.

2. Moved my critique across institutions with dizzying speed, where it jumped political and professional barriers.

3. Offered direct access to influential individuals who read their own e-mail as well as to an amusing gallery of quirky cyberspace characters.

4. Fueled the controversy through the immediate and uncensored publication of vivid commentary and speculation.

5. Created new and intriguing issues for cyberspace debate that went beyond the original MIT controversy.

6. Offered the fun of a free-for-all where passions and imagination could rage.

In this chapter, I briefly summarize the content of the "MIT Study on the Status of Women." Second, I discuss the difficulty of mounting a challenge to the MIT study outside cyberspace. Third, I discuss the different nature of scientific debate in cyberspace as opposed to the restrained and time-lagged discussions of professional journals.

The MIT Study on the Status of Women Faculty in Science at MIT: The Claims and the Critique

"In the summer of 1994, three tenured women faculty in the School of Science began to discuss the quality of their professional lives at

MIT," begins the MIT study. "In the course of their careers these women had come to realize that gender had probably caused their professional lives to differ significantly from those of their male colleagues.... It was soon clear to the women that their experiences formed a pattern."

The particular incident that sparked these discussions was a demand for additional laboratory space by Professor Nancy Hopkins in the Biology Department. A second grievance was the alleged takeover of a course she had taught by a male professor, who was producing a CD-ROM related to the course.

Professor Hopkins believed she was the victim of sex discrimination and consulted an attorney who advised her to complain to the MIT administration. After mobilizing other senior women in the School of Science at MIT, Professor Hopkins and her allies met with Robert J. Birgeneau, then Dean of the School of Science, to discuss their grievances.

Dean Birgeneau appointed a committee to look into the charges of gender discrimination. To chair the committee, he appointed Nancy Hopkins herself, the chief complainant. Two-thirds of the committee members were senior women, interested parties to the dispute. This first committee operated from 1995 to 1997 and produced the major report purporting to find gender discrimination. A second committee was appointed in 1997, chaired by MIT Professor Mary C. Potter, and senior women again comprised two-thirds of the committee, thus forming a voting majority.

The Committee claims to have examined sex differences in laboratory space, salaries (the report says that primary salary data were denied the committee although the impression is given that salaries were examined), allocation of internal research funds, and other resources. The Committee also interviewed both the senior women at the School of Science and the untenured junior women. Their findings: MIT was guilty of unintentional gender discrimination.

To summarize briefly the points I make in a twenty-three-page critique of the MIT study:

1. The senior women at MIT were judge and jury of their own complaints. Those judging the charge of discrimination stood to benefit from a finding of discrimination, and did benefit. According to media reports, Nancy Hopkins received a substantial salary raise, a spacious new laboratory, and millions of dollars in MIT's internally allocated research funds. "No man is allowed to be a judge in his own case," James Madison pointed out in Federalist Papers #10, "because his interest would certainly bias his judgment, and not improbably, corrupt his integrity. " MIT did not hesitate to make a woman the judge of her own case.

2. The MIT study kept the facts secret, claiming that "confidentiality" is required when it comes to publishing tables on such trivial matters as sex differences in square feet of laboratory space. Since the names of the female faculty in the School of Science are readily available from the MIT catalog, the argument that the data must be kept confidential is absurd. Science depends on the reporting of the data on which claims are based.

Secret data invites the speculation that no sex differences were actually found, and such rumors were rife at MIT. Indeed, a highly placed confidential source at MIT, willing to speak only under the protection of anonymity, says that the Committee on the Status of Women actually found no sex differences:

> Heroic efforts were made to get statistics but a lot of this information was hard to gather, like who had what space. There was insufficient data from any of these sources to determine anything in particular.
>
> Nobody can make judgments anyway with such small numbers of people doing such totally different things.

3. Even perceptions of sex discrimination among MIT's female faculty were far from universal. Always read the appendix. We learn therein that junior women faculty felt that they were treated equally, although they were concerned about such issues as work and family balance. Since no numbers are provided, we do not know whether this is "all" or "most" junior women. The numbers are confusing as to how many of the senior women felt marginalized—no coding system or counts are presented. Nor does the report acknowledge what a reporter later found—one prominent senior faculty member, physicist June Matthews, resigned from the first committee. While some of the complaints were legitimate, she said, most of the issues were a lot of "hype and hysteria." She later claimed she was misquoted.

4. The claims by the senior women in the School of Science that, as "pioneers" in science, they are "exceptional" or even equal in scientific accomplishments to the male faculty are untrue. The claim of gender discrimination rests on a crucial assumption: that the senior women at MIT are the equal of the senior men in scientific stature. Thus, any difference in favor of men in resources or rewards is evidence of gender discrimination, as opposed to a just distribution based on merit.

Not only does the "MIT Study on the Status of Women" fail to address the obvious question when it comes to considering gender differences in salary or resources of whether the senior female faculty at MIT were equal to the senior male faculty in scientific stature. Even to raise the question, asserts the report, brands the inquirer as a bigot:

> Once and for all we must recognize that the heart and soul of discrimination, the last refuge of the bigot, is to say that those who are discriminated against deserve it because they are less good.

Such overheated rhetoric and before-the-fact accusations hide the evidence. As I previously discussed, two independent researchers found that the MIT senior female faculty in the Biology Department were dramatically less productive than the senior men.

Despite the original MIT's report innocence of evidence, the *New York Times* published an editorial on March 28, 1999 stating that

> Hard evidence of this phenomenon (gender bias) is found in a new report on women on the science faculty of the Massachusetts Institute of Technology....the study has significant social value because it documents with unusual clarity how pervasive and destructive discrimination can be even when there is no blatant harassment or intimidation.

Media Response to the MIT Study and the Difficulty of Mounting a Critique

The mainstream media embraced the MIT Study on the Status of Women uncritically. "MIT Admits Discrimination Against Female Professors" shouted the headline of a front page story in the *New York Times* on March 23, 1999. The ensuing media blitz brought virtually universal applause for Professor Hopkins and for MIT's brave *mea culpa*. Professor Hopkins was invited to the White House where the President and Mrs. Clinton praised her for her courage. She received a substantial increase in salary, additional research funds, and was hastily admitted as a member to the National Academy of Science's Institute of Medicine.

Attempts to provide balance to the story were notable for their absence, but the fault was not entirely with the press. Few at MIT would talk about it. *USA Today* noted on July 27, 1999, that male faculty at MIT have remained publicly silent. Robin Wilson in the *Chronicle of Higher Education* did succeed in finding contrary opinion, quoting briefly at the conclusion of the *Chronicle*'s cover story, Professor Daniel Kleitman, a member of the original investigatory committee, who said he saw no gender discrimination in the committee's review of the evidence. But the main theme in the mainstream press was the triumph of Nancy Hopkins and the suffering sisterhood and the salvation of MIT through confession of sin and redemptive redress.

I had no particular interest in the MIT study on the status of women when the Independent Women's Forum, where I am a member of the national advisory board, asked me to take a look at it as a public service. My father had gone to MIT so I was curious about what was going on at the school. I was skeptical of the media stories reporting gender discrimination but then I would have been skeptical had the media reported the opposite—that no gender discrimination was found at MIT. Were I to undertake a study of the issue of gender discrimination in academia, my working hypothesis would be that the situation is complex. Competing forces are at work: some old-fashioned sexism and unconscious stereotyping, some blatant affirmative action in favor of women, uncertainty about what kinds of personal remarks are pleasantries and what kinds are out-of-bounds, and an atmosphere of intellectual McCarthyism that prevents honest analysis of the issues.

Whether or not gender discrimination did or did not exist at MIT, anyone examining the MIT study would conclude that this study was not science. The problem was how to expose it. Why would the media pick up the story? A professor at a university in Fairbanks, Alaska publishes a study challenging the Massachusetts Institute of Technology with no new data. No news hook? This is hardly a story worth reporting.

My counter-report, released on December 14, 1999, at a discussion of gender issues at the American Enterprise Institute, at first languished. In his syndicated column in *U.S. News and World Report* on December 20, 1999, John Leo did devote his column to the issue, making the point that "the authors of modern bias reports no longer feel compelled to present actual evidence. Thanks to the cooperation of the mainstream press, a vague but loud accusation is more than enough to land you on Page 1."

Otherwise I was ignored. To my knowledge, no major American newspaper with the exception of the *Wall Street Journal* mentioned my critique. This was not for want of effort. I had sent a copy of the critique with e-mail notes to many of the journalists who had covered the original MIT story. No response came from MIT—the matter was beneath notice and would soon blow over.

To her credit, Constance Holden, a veteran reporter at *Science*, did see an obligation to report a critique on scientific grounds. *Science*, after all, had published on November 12, 1999, a lengthy story lauding MIT—its tone best captured by the caption under the photograph of MIT's Dean Birgeneau: "Hero." But Holden's editors thought the critique worth only a squib.

While the mainstream media buried the story, a national controversy ignited in cyberspace. The kindling was a news bullet published on the Internet: Robin Wilson, who covers gender issues at the *Chronicle of Higher Education,* published a short summary of my critique in the on-line edition of the *Chronicle*. This newsletter arrives as a daily bulletin in the e-mail of administrators and faculty members across the nation.

To cut and paste this *Chronicle* news bullet onto a new e-mail message and shoot it to colleagues in cyberspace took only a moment. The critics of the original MIT study, seeing vindication in this new study, could inform their friends and allies that the Emperor had been shot at without taking time, responsibility, or risk. Advocates of the original MIT study had to warn their own allies that the Emperor was in danger. Anyone could check out both the original MIT study and my critique with ease—both were published on the Web.

The *Chronicle* news bullet reporting my critique zipped around in cyberspace. Both allies and adversaries posted it on listservs and sent it to their friends. A professor at a technical university who was sympathetic to my critique, for example, sent the story to the provost of MIT and to other MIT faculty with personal notes, as well as to administrators at his own institution expressing the hope that his institution would not repeat MIT's folly. Through dense and tangled social networks, the story bounced from profession to profession—to psychologists, educators, lawyers, building contractors. The study jumped the political spectrum, from such anti-affirmative action groups as "Americans Against Discriminations and Preferences" to such feminist groups as the "Women's Studies Association." The study crossed oceans to universities in Europe, New Zealand, and Australia. I began to receive forwarded messages urging me to respond to a critique that had appeared on this list or that. Once I caught on to the dissemination vectors, I began to use them strategically. I urged an e-mail correspondent in Europe, for example, who told me that the issue of gender in science was invading European universities, to post an announcement of my critique on relevant European listservs.

A central problem in any battle is maintaining morale. Had this controversy been limited to the mainstream media or to academic journals, where critiques and responses take many months to publish, I might quickly have lost heart and lost interest. Cyberspace communication, on the other hand, meant that every day my e-mail box was bursting with messages of support and condemnation—an immediate reinforcement to continue the fight.

I was astonished to learn how many people knew of my critique, even though the mainstream press had for the most part ignored the story. On one occasion, I read a newspaper story lauding MIT and denouncing the provost of one of America's top universities who was resisting a copycat response. I sent him an e-mail intended to let him know of my critique. But he already knew about it, he said, in a reply I received less than two hours later. Cyberspace communication, I learned, offers personal access: provosts, professors of international repute, even a Nobel prize winner—all read and responded to their own e-mail.

I also met a gallery of cyberspace characters who offered additional information on the issues: a workman at MIT who gave me a remarkably hands-on opinion on the laboratory facilities afforded female faculty; a renowned professor who corrected an error, offered an inside detail, and explained why he was not in a position to respond; a graduate student who offered to get the blueprints of MIT's offices and labs and assess claims of gender unfairness with his own tape measure; the head of a gender equity program who posted a three page, single-space critique of my study on the Women's Studies list but would participate in no discussion; a feminist who was also skeptical of my study but was willing to engage in a dialogue which modified both of our views until we called a halt for the holidays.

I even met in cyberspace a "double" who amplified my own intellectual capacity. She was a colleague of the same age and ethnicity, who shared my judgment about the MIT study but who was more adept at computer detective work and who was more knowledgeable about certain areas of the relevant research. After corresponding in cyberspace, we arranged to meet. "You will be able to recognize me," she said, "because I don't look like a victim." When we met, I did a double take: we had dressed in identical black pants suits with identical folk jewelry necklaces. Thereafter, we corresponded several times a day by e-mail on the MIT issue. The incident is amusing but brings up an important point: Cyberspace creates community and the social support needed for a lonely battle.

Cyberspace communication was also just plain fun. You met strange characters, like the anonymous "La Griffe du Lion" (the mane of the lion), who published a web journal offering mathematically sophisticated but politically incorrect analyses of discrimination. When I asked him why he refused to identify himself, he replied, "There is a certain purity in anonymity. In the world of the anonymous there are no experts and no gods. Nobel laureates are no better than their arguments."

Entering cyberspace I felt like Alice in Wonderland, wondering just who would turn up next—a caterpillar with a hookah, a grin from a Cheshire cat, old Father William standing on his head.

The cyberspace debate was also invigorating for my critics. "What a great break from reading exams," said one of my antagonists on the Women's Studies List. "I grade better when I'm mad."

I would like to measure the number of people my critique reached in cyberspace, but the number is virtually impossible to ascertain. The crucial measurements are the numbers of people who become (1) aware that the issue exists; (2) knowledgeable about the thesis through actually reading the message; or (3) informed of the arguments through reading the linked report. In my experience, people do not open many of the messages they receive from e-mail lists, although they usually glance at the subject line to see if the message is worth opening. A subject line which packs in the point, such as "MIT Tarnishes Its Reputation with Junk Gender Science," delivers the punch even if the message lies unopened.

While I cannot offer an estimate of cyberspace audience, I can provide a few examples of the readership of sites where my critique of MIT appeared:

- *Education News.* Jimmy Kilpatrick, the editor, says that this vigorous site averages 8-10,000 hits a day. "The majority of education, public policy, and world-wide and US education news writers are on our mailing list."

- *Women's Studies List*. According to site information, WMST-L is an "international electronic forum for people involved in Women's Studies. The list now has more than four thousand subscribers in forty-seven countries, ranging from the United States and Canada to Israel, Saudi Arabia, Brazil, Singapore, and Australia."

- *PsychWatch*. According to site information, this list has over 12,000 readers in sixty-eight countries.

- *Center/Right*. This is an e-newsletter of centrist, conservative, and libertarian ideas which targets the legal profession and has more than 2,500 subscribers.

The most vigorous discussion occurred on small lists with intense interest in matters of political correctness, discrimination and preferences. One e-mail correspondent told me that the notice of the study printed in the *Chronicle* was bouncing all over Harvard and MIT.

Although I have no way of verifying the accuracy of this claim, one revealing incident suggests its plausibility. In December 1999, CNN called to ask me to appear on *CNN&Time*, hosted by Bernard Shaw and Jeff Greenfield. The show had scheduled a segment on bias at MIT. The next day CNN called back to cancel saying that Professor Nancy Hopkins, who had previously agreed to appear, had canceled because of "all the controversy." The cyberspace controversy had thus turned my critique into national news.

When I entered "Judith Kleinfeld MIT" into the Google search engine in August, 2001, I found 230 hits. While MIT and the mainstream press chose to bury their heads in the sand, debate on the Internet was raging, and this debate took a different character than debate in scientific journals or in the press.

Differences in the Debate in the Mainstream Media and in Cyberspace

In a nutshell, debate in cyberspace was far more open and entertaining than debate in the mainstream media. The pieces published in letters to the editor columns had a formal, labored quality to them. The letter writers were very much aware that they were speaking for the record. Some complained that their published letters had been edited so as to misrepresent and "ding them." In cyberspace, in contrast, debate raged and ranged, exploring new dimensions of the issues such as:

- *Moral Courage*: The cyberspace dialogue sheds a revealing light on the silencing of dissent when feminist issues are in play. Many e-mail correspondents told me that they too knew that the MIT Study did not meet minimal scientific standards, but they feared expressing an opinion in public. Untenured professors feared their careers would be in jeopardy:

  > Unfortunately, many men think that they'll be ostracized for their candor; Men in academia CAN'T write what you did, for fear of reprisal...

But even male faculty with tenure feared the damage to their reputations should they speak out on such an emotional issue:

> The problem is, If I were to attempt such a paper, it would be dismissed as the ravings of one more patriarchal male desperate to retain the reins of power.

To be labeled as "having a problem with women" reduces career prospects, and the men knew it. Advocacy on feminist issues, on the other hand, can advance career prospects. As a visible case in point, the MIT Study on the Status of Women helped MIT's Dean Birgeneau obtain the presidency of the University of Toronto, Canada's leading university. Before he even took office, he made clear the costs to University of Toronto faculty of disagreeing with him. Although later complaining that he had been misquoted, he was reported in the *Toronto Star* to have warned University of Toronto administrators that "diversity is one of the high priorities that I expected everybody in the leadership position at the university to be committed to." His message was clear: If you don't agree with my position on diversity, step down.

A particularly sad commentary came from a distinguished professor who had fought similar battles in an earlier era:

> I ask them, what is there to be brave about? I am a tenured professor and taking no risk whatever. Some people may not like what I say, be angry with me, but is that something for a grown person to shun?

Yet even he preferred to avoid a fight with feminists and gave me permission to quote him only anonymously. He was tired, he explained, and he didn't want to deal with the "boring repercussions."

In short, people were far more likely to speak out in cyberspace than in a print forum. Still, let me be clear about the effects of the intellectual McCarthyism pervading academia on feminist issues. *Honest reporters, who wanted to report fairly on the other side of the MIT story, complained that they could not do so when virtually no one would speak for attribution.*

- *The Rage of Aggrieved Elites:* As people tried to make sense of the events at MIT, the cyberspace debate spun off into new areas. *Science* reporter Constance Holden, for example, posed this question:

My initial reaction to the MIT report was one of skepticism, but after reading Andrew Lawler's article I became persuaded that they had actually experienced a lot of anguish. It doesn't make sense to me that a woman who had achieved tenure at MIT—which especially if the environment is "chilly" would entail a lot of toughness—would suddenly turn into a crybaby.

I sent her query to cyberspace colleagues who offered their own answers. Administrators pointed out that faculty, male and female, are always comparing their own situation to others whom they see as better off, and such complaints among star senior professors were far from unusual. Kevin Kilty, an adjunct engineering professor, pointed out the MIT women did not appreciate their good fortune:

The tales of woe profiled in *Science* were not unlike the woes that many male faculty suffer; and the actual women profiled seemed unlike real victims. The woman astronomer in particular makes cameo appearances on NOVA and the Discovery Channel, has weighty titles, an esteemed position that allows her to do great science and has won prestigious awards. I can only imagine such treatment; while she nurses resentments.

Why such rage among "aggrieved elites?" asked Jonathan Imber, editor of *Society*, in a speculative e-mail. "It is interesting how much the culture of reparations has come to obsess elites in this country."

The Elites Strike Back

The power of the Internet to open up debate has not gone unnoticed by the "aggrieved elites." In a counter-attack, University of Chicago law professor Cass Sunstein makes the argument that technology has made it possible for people to "filter" what they want to be exposed to. "In the long run, the most serious 'digital divides' might involve numerous free-speech enclaves, effectively walled off from each other," says Sunstein in a March, 2001 article in the *Chronicle of Higher Education* adapted from his new book *Republic.com.* This is a peculiar comment from so distinguished a professor. The debate between the left and the right in this country is a dialogue, a tennis game where neither side can play without the other. I could not critique the MIT study, for example, without reporting the study itself and its findings. The Internet, this case example suggests, creates a world of free and vigorous discussion and debate which crosses political and professional boundaries. This is not to ignore the problem of mis-information on Internet sources. But the classic remedy for false speech is more speech. The Internet creates a world where the media elite do not reign, where free speech flourishes, and so does democracy.

References

American Association of University Women Educational Foundation, *Gender Gaps: Where Schools Still Fail Our Children*, Washington, DC: American Association of University Women, 1998.

David C. Geary, *Male, Female: The Evolution of Human Sex Differences*, American Psychological Association, 1998.

Patricia Hausman and James Steiger, "Confession without Guilt?" Washington, D.C. Independent Women's Forum, 2001.

Dorothy Kimura, *Sex and Cognition*, Cambridge, MA: Massachusetts Institute of Technology, 1999.

Judith Kleinfeld, "Student Performance: Males versus Females," *Public Interest*, Winter (1999), pp. 3-20.

Judith Kleinfeld, "MIT Tarnishes Its Reputation with Junk Gender Science. Arlington," VA: Independent Women's Forum, 1999 at http://www.uaf.edu/northern/mitstudy/

"The MIT Study on the Status of Women Faculty." *MIT Faculty Newsletter*, (March 1999) at http://web.mit.edu/fnl/women/women.html.

Andrew Lawler,"Tenured Women Battle to Make It Less Lonely at the Top," *Science* 286 (November 12, 1999), p. 1273.

Kathryn Jean Lopez, "Glass Ceilings and Foggy Science," *Heterodoxy*. February-March, 2000.

David Lubinski and Camilla Benbow, "Gender Differences in Abilities and Preferences Among the Gifted: Implications for the Math-Science Pipeline," *Current Directions in Psychological Science*, 1 (1992), pp. 61-66.

Scott Smallwood, "Report Questions Methodology and Conclusions of MIT Gender-Discrimination Study," *Chronicle of Higher Education*, February 7, 2001.

Christina Hoff Sommers, *Who Stole Feminism?* New York: Simon & Schuster, 1994.

Cass Sunstein, *Republic.com*. Princeton, NJ: Princeton University Press, 2001.

Robin Wilson. "An MIT Professor's Suspicion of Bias Leads to a New Movement for Academic Women," *The Chronicle of Higher Education*, (December 3, 1999), A16-A18.

3

American Distortion of Dutch Drug Statistics

Robert J. MacCoun

In early 1998, I published an essay in the *Annual Review of Psychology* on bias in the interpretation and use of social science research evidence by researchers and research consumers. In many ways, it was a discouraging essay, documenting the numerous psychological, sociological, and economic processes that can produce such biases, and the increasing evidence that they can occur unintentionally as a result of otherwise adaptive cognitive mechanisms.

But the idea that such biases are pervasive is already widely held—if anything, the public probably errs on the side of excessive skepticism of experts. So the essay offered some arguments against cynicism. First, under standard decision theory analyses, "biased" interpretation of evidence is sometimes normatively justifiable. Second, recent research indicates that credible counter-evidence does tend to curtail extreme claims in favor of one's position—we do not simply see whatever we want in the data. And third, we should avoid jumping to quick conclusions about experts' motives. It is devilishly difficult to establish that someone else is being biased—indeed, the bias is often in the eye of the beholder. The "hostile media phenomenon" provides evidence for this last point. In many conflicts, it has been shown that each side of a dispute tends to think that the media is biased in favor of the other side.

Ironically, after completing that essay, but before it appeared in print, I was confronted with two examples of what seemed to be gross distortions of my own recent research on Dutch cannabis policies and outcomes. In my gut, all my earlier talk of normative justification, data-constrained assertions, and biased beholders seemed like so much hooey. Two years later I am still trying to reconcile my intellect and my gut.

Dutch cannabis policy is a staple of the U.S. drug policy debate, because it the closest thing to drug legalization in a modern industrialized nation—for drugs other than tobacco and alcohol. Since 1976, the Dutch have maintained a formal legal prohibition on cannabis products (marijuana and hashish), while tolerating the commercial sales of up to 30 grams of cannabis (reduced to 5 grams in 1995), mostly in coffee shops and bars. "Toleration" does not mean discretionary non-enforcement, like the casual way Americans police prostitution or illicit gambling. It means that there are formal written policies instructing the police and prosecutors not to enforce cannabis prohibition for small quantity transactions.

(Drug) War Story

In October 1997, Peter Reuter and I published an article in *Science* examining Dutch "de facto" cannabis legalization and its consequences. The article was motivated by our frustration with the grossly discrepant "factual" comparisons of U.S. and Dutch drug statistics routinely encountered in the mass media and on the internet. According to recent clippings in our files, the lifetime prevalence of marijuana use (the percentage who have ever used marijuana) among Dutch teens had either fallen from 15 to 2 percent or risen from 5 to 14 percent. Readers were told that respective marijuana rates for Dutch and U.S. adolescents were either 14 vs. 38 percent or 30 vs. 11 percent.

The sources of these factoids appear authoritative on their face, and in fact each is technically accurate. It all depends on which statistics one cites—in particular, the year of the estimate and the age group of the respondents. Even under the best of circumstances, cross-national comparisons are problematic. But at the very least, one ought to compare rates for the same year, and the same age groups.

Reuter and I set out to describe more accurately Dutch policies and outcomes and assess what lessons, if any, they plausibly provided for the U.S. drug debate. Our article presented time-series data on cannabis prevalence over a twenty-five-year period in the Netherlands, and fifteen static comparisons of Dutch and non-Dutch (American, Danish, and or German) cannabis prevalence rates, each matched by age group and year.

Our interpretation of the Dutch data was rather nuanced, so we crafted a carefully worded press release, designed to minimize potential misunderstandings. On 3 October 1997, the day *Science* lifted the embargo, we were pleased to discover that our study was widely covered. Many papers, including *USA Today* and the *San Francisco Chronicle*, ran an Associated Press story by Paul Recer. Our delight turned to dismay when we read the following passages: "... the percentage of 18-year-olds who had tried marijuana rose from 15 percent to 44 percent" in the Netherlands, but "by contrast, teenage use of marijuana in the United States was estimated at about 12 percent in 1992."

The Recer article implied a 32 percent difference between the two nations, clearly implying that there are a lot more stoned Dutch teens than U.S. teens. In fact, according to our paper, there were three possible comparisons between matched national estimates from the Netherlands and the United States, and they had "an average Dutch-U.S. difference of 1%, well within the sampling error of the surveys."

We immediately submitted a correction letter to the Associated Press and to each paper that ran the Recer story. The key passage explains how Recer's selective facts distorted our article: "This comparison, which is not taken from our article...is quite misleading, for two reasons. First, it compares the lifetime experience of Dutch 18-year-olds to that of all U.S. teens. But in each country, 18-year-olds are much more likely to have tried marijuana than other teens, because they have lived longer, and because drug experimentation is more common in late adolescence. Second, it compares a 1996 Dutch rate with a 1992 U.S. rate, yet U.S. rates skyrocketed between 1992 and 1996." Our account was precise, but tedious, which may explain why it was only published in one paper, the *Honolulu Advertiser*. We were gratified by that correction, but had aspired to bring truth to light in all fifty states, or at least some of the lower forty-eight.

Significantly, Recer's Dutch figure appeared in our press release; the U.S. figure did not. The correct U.S. figure for 12 to 17-year-olds in 1996, 10.6 percent, was described by Recer as "around 12 percent," suggesting he got it from some different source. Indeed, we suspect he never saw our article, basing his story entirely on the press release. A call to Recer produced neither a correction nor any clarification. He seemed not to see why there was a problem, arguing that eighteen-year-olds are in fact teenagers. (I asked rhetorically: Would he compare the average height of eighteen-year-olds to that of twelve-to-seventeen year-olds?)

Almost a year later, in July of 1998, we were cited in a *Los Angeles Times* op-ed essay by General Barry McCaffrey, the director of the Office of National Drug Control Policy (ONDCP). He wrote, "A 1997 study by Robert MacCoun and Peter Reuter...notes that the percentage of Dutch 18-year-olds who tried pot rose from 15 percent to 34 percent from 1984 to 1992, a time when the numbers weren't climbing in other European nations. By contrast, in 1992 teenage use of marijuana in the United States was estimated at 10.6 percent." It appeared that the Associated Press story had taken on a life of its own.

We were at least heartened to see the 32 percent gap reduced to 24 percent, though still well above the correct 1 to 2 percent difference we had reported. Apparently, on the basis of a phone conversation with my co-author, the ONDCP staff corrected the 1992-1996 discrepancy but failed to correct the eighteen vs. twelve-to-seventeen age discrepancy.

We wrote a correction letter to the *Los Angeles Times*, and faxed a copy to ONDCP as a courtesy. They immediately contacted us to apologize, and we negotiated an arrangement whereby we would withdraw our correction letter and ONDCP would correct the error themselves. We received a copy of that letter but it never appeared in the *Times*. Some months later, the *Houston Chronicle* ran the McCaffrey essay in its uncorrected form. A call to ONDCP elicited another agreement that they would send in a correction. Again, no correction letter was ever published.

This was not the first time General McCaffrey had mischaracterized Dutch policy. Earlier that same month, in a critique of Dutch tolerance toward hard drug users, he asserted that the Dutch homicide rate was over twice that of the U.S., when in fact the U.S. rate (8 per 100,000) is four times larger than the Dutch rate (1.8 per 100,000). The erroneous figures were based on an apparent failure to realize that the Dutch statistics included unsuccessful homicide attempts.

My essay on biased interpretation relied heavily on a key distinction in contemporary social and cognitive psychology—hot vs. cold cognition. Cold cognition is abstract and dispassionate, but not necessarily "rational"—it is nearly as vulnerable to distortion, but due to the "quick and dirty" mechanical shortcuts of mental processing. Hot cognition is cognition infused with emotion and motivation. For several months after these media incidents, my own interpretations were positively scalding. With the passage of time, I'm now able to reflect on these events more coolly.

War stories like mine are all too common in the public debate on American drug policy, as they are in many other areas of social policy. Are they inevitable? Are they defensible?

Interpreting Misinterpretations

Arguably, there are at least two normatively justifiable mechanisms for "biased" interpretation of evidence. First, from the standpoint of the Bayesian induction framework, disagreements about the *a posteriori* probability of a hypothesis, conditioned on the available data, are justifiable when judges differ in their "priors"—their subjective estimate of the *a priori* probability of the hypothesis. Second, because evidence strength is a matter of degree, the dichotomous decision to accept or reject a verdict requires a decision threshold or standard of proof. Decision theory suggests that perceivers can and should apply different thresholds depending on their relative aversion to false positive errors (accepting a hypothesis when it is false) vs. false negative errors (rejecting it when it is true).

But it is unclear how one might exonerate the distortions in the AP story and the McCaffrey essay on these normative grounds. These sources did not simply differ from our *Science* essay in their judgment of the likely effect of policy differences on Dutch vs. U.S. drug rates, or on the question of whether the weight of the evidence favored one policy approach over the other. Rather, they simply juxtaposed correct facts in a manner that is charitably described as meaningless, and less charitably described as patently misleading.

What of the argument that one should be wary of labeling others as biased? Admittedly, I am hardly capable of cool neutrality in my assessment of these uses of my research. But to assert, as I do, that Recer and McCaffrey distorted the evidence is not to impute motives or assert that they acted fraudulently. Recer's error might be viewed as deceptive, but it might simply reflect confusion or carelessness. For General McCaffrey's essay, a plausible account might invoke an overworked staff, a recent public history of skepticism if not outright hostility toward the Dutch approach to drug problems, and an AP story that seemed to meet their rhetorical needs.

Cynicism and Hope

After some decades debating hot vs. cold accounts of various judgmental biases, most psychologists have come to the conclusion that "warm cognition" is the norm. Warm cognition is motivated—it acts in the service of furthering one's desired ends. But it acts the way lawyers are supposed to act when they are properly fulfilling their advocacy role. Evidence constrains warm cognition; we cannot simply claim to see whatever we want to see. Social psychologists call this "constrained directional bias"—we push our interpretation as far in the desired direction as the evidence will permit, but not further. Evidence against our positions gets scrutinized with a fine-toothed comb; evidence that can plausibly be construed as favorable is immediately flaunted.

A corollary to the "constrained directional bias" idea is the suggestion by Harry Kalven and Hans Zeisel, in their 1966 *The American Jury,* that jurors' personal sentiments are most likely to emerge as a factor in deliberations when the evidence was equivocal or ambiguous. Similarly, physicist and science fiction author Gregory Benford has offered a "Law of Controversy" in which "passion is inversely proportional to the amount of real information available."

Drug policy fits these models perfectly. For many if not most Americans, the use of intoxicating drugs, at least illegal ones, is a profoundly immoral act and must be judged and policed on moral terms. In principle, illicit drugs might be regulated like any other risky activity, and one can plausibly argue that doing so might produce more effective policies than the current approach. But the fact of the matter is that the science of drug policy is still remarkably crude. At present, there is little serious prospect of the sort of demonstrably effective technical expertise that might trump simple moral intuitions—as has largely happened in the domains of medicine, cosmology, and (for the most part) natural history.

Will good drug data eventually drive out misleading claims? There are some grounds for optimism. In various domains, policy-relevant indictors—macroeconomic, agricultural, educational—are now routinely collected in a standardized fashion by highly trained technicians using state-of-the-art methods for establishing reliability and validity. Gradually, slowly, American drug data collection and analysis is moving in this general direction. There are various efforts in Western Europe to standardize the collection and reporting of statistics on drug use and drug-related outcomes. And a favorable sign is that even the most extremely partisan drug warrior and drug reformer web sites now provide links to the web pages of the major government drug data sources.

Relatively good data are already widely available on American crime and criminal sanctioning rates, at least in comparison to the poor state of drug statistics. Local politicians take credit for falling crime rates, and blame others for rising crime rates, but they rarely assert that rates are falling when they are rising. Nevertheless, distortion is still rampant in criminal justice discourse. Systematic content analyses show that the media disproportionately reports the most heinous, atypical crimes, and the "cops" on live-action shows are disproportionately white and the offenders are disproportionately black.

Science and Conflicting Values

The misrepresentations of our research resulted in part from a questionable assumption—the notion that one can assess the relative merits of American vs. Dutch approaches to the drug problem by comparing current marijuana rates in each country. This exemplifies the "horse race" reflex in American journalism and politics.

Recent levels of Dutch and American marijuana use are roughly equal, a fact that drug war doves find congenial because drug war hawks believe tolerance should raise drug rates. But we found the changes in Dutch use over time more informative. In the early 1970s, Dutch cannabis rates were considerably lower than those in the U.S., and they remained at that low level for at least a decade after the 1976 Dutch drug law. But Dutch use rose steeply during the 1980s, coinciding with a rapid increase in the number and visibility of the cannabis coffee shops. We argued that the experience of the first decade suggests that depenalizing possession, *per se,* produces little or no measurable increase in drug use. On the other hand, we hypothesized that commercial promotion, not surprisingly, produces a significant increase in the market for cannabis.

Thus, even without distortion, our article already offered something for each side of the debate. As a result, most subsequent citations of our article have been accurate, but selective. For example, in February 1998, an article in *New Scientist* correctly cited our conclusion that "reductions in criminal penalties have little effect on drug use, at least for marijuana." The April 1998 issue printed a letter from a British government official objecting to this "seriously misleading quotation from the editorial summary of [MacCoun and Reuter's] article," which, he noted, actually said that "growth in commercial access to cannabis, after de facto legalization, was accompanied by steep increases in use, even among youth." The editors replied by quoting our methodological caveat that the correlation between rising marijuana use and the increasing number of coffee shops "may not be causal."

Technically, each statement in this exchange is accurate. Taken separately, each draws a different lesson from the Dutch experience; each is incomplete. Improvements in drug statistics seem unlikely to eliminate this sort of selective emphasis. Accuracy will invariably breed consensus. When accurate portrayals depict a complex world, conflicting values can always yield conflicting simplifications.

4

Science in *A Civil Action*

Allan Mazur

By comparing court cases in which science has been used well with cases where it has been used poorly, we may learn how better to incorporate scientific evidence into litigation. A case worthy of study involves the cluster of childhood leukemia cases in Woburn, Massachusetts made famous by writer Jonathan Harr whose bestseller, *A Civil Action* (Random House, 1995), describes a suit by the aggrieved parents against two large corporations, W.R. Grace and Beatrice Foods, alleged to be responsible for the leukemias. The Woburn case has by now been studied by several investigators who, like Harr, were not themselves parties to the litigation, leaving us a trove of research illuminating the role of science during the trial.

The Water

Prior to the 1960s Woburn used six pumps (Wells A to F) to draw its drinking water from an underground aquifer in the western part of the city. Needing an additional supply, the city began to exploit an aquifer in east Woburn, opening Well G in 1964 and Well H in 1967. Wells G and H stand 600 feet apart near the narrow Aberjona River, which runs atop the east aquifer. These new wells served homes in the eastern part of the city, and to a lesser extent in the north and central sections but not in western Woburn.

The new water was not totally satisfactory. In 1967 the state required it to be chlorinated because of its poor bacterial quality. The water had a funny taste, perhaps because of the chlorine, and it was brown from dissolved iron and manganese, discoloring clothing and dishwashers. Dissatisfied citizens organized in 1969 to force the mayor to close Wells G and H. As a result the wells were usually shut off, but during periods of summer drought they would be restarted to make up the shortfall in water.

Anne Anderson and her husband moved to Woburn in 1965, purchasing a home on the east side of the city serviced by the new wells. She complained about the tap water to the city board of health and the public works department (Harr, pp. 21-24). In 1972 the Andersons' young son Jimmie was diagnosed with acute lymphocytic leukemia (ALL), finally dying in 1981. During the agonizing years of Jimmie's illness, Anne Anderson became aware of other children with leukemia in her neighborhood and wondered if the drinking water was to blame.

After Love Canal became a national news story in 1978, the American public began to worry about toxic chemical waste, which heretofore had not been of much concern. An ABC documentary exemplifies the publicity given this problem: "The Killing Ground" was televised on March 29, 1979, with segments on Love Canal and on illegal "midnight dumping" of toxic waste. Woburn would be lifted upward by this rising tide of media attention. In April 1979 a reporter for the Woburn *Daily Times* noticed a police report about midnight dumping of 184 barrels near the Aberjona River and notified authorities that Wells G and H were nearby. The state tested water samples from the wells and found high concentrations of the common industrial solvents trichloroethylene (TCE) and perchloroethylene (PCE). It was later found that the illegally dumped barrels contained harmless polyurethane, not the solvents found in the wells. But TCE and PCE were listed by the Environmental Protection Agency as "probable" carcinogens so the state closed the wells.

On September 10, 1979, the *Daily Times* reported the discovery near a hundred-year-old industrial complex in north Woburn of an abandoned lagoon in which arsenic had been disposed. It was unclear if the metal had contaminated Wells G and H, situated a mile to the south, according to the news story, but it noted that the wells had already been closed because of contamination with TCE.

Anne Anderson, speaking in a PBS television documentary, "Toxic Trials," made in 1986 for the PBS television program, *Nova*, said when she heard of the well contamination,

> It was just like a click in my mind—that's what it is. I could never be convinced after that—nobody could convince me—that the contamination of that water was not causing our problem.

Anderson and her minister announced in the *Daily Times* a meeting for all parents who had had a child diagnosed with leukemia in the past fifteen years, producing information on twelve cases. Perhaps modeling their approach on the activities at Love Canal, they plotted the leukemias on a map—a kind of analysis sociologist Phil Brown, in his account of the Woburn story, *No Safe Place* (University of California Press, 1997), has called "barefoot epidemiology." Eight of twelve identified cases were in east Woburn, and six clustered in Anderson's own neighborhood.

In 1980 the Centers for Disease Control studied the cluster and concluded that the leukemia incidence in east Woburn was at least seven times greater than expected (and normal in the rest of the city). Cluster investigations almost invariably fail to find a common cause, not because one does not exist, but because potential causes— chemicals, radiation, infectious agents—are so poorly understood, and the number of cluster cases is so small, that it is nearly impossible to produce a statistically incriminating result. Here, as usual, the CDC found no potential cause that was common to the victims and differentiated them from a control group. The distribution pattern of water from Wells G and H, not well known at that time, was not explicitly considered in the study. The CDC and the EPA both noted that the contaminants in the well water were not known to cause leukemia.

Some of the parents began to discuss the water theory with lawyers in 1980. At the time there was still nothing beyond intuition to implicate the wells, and the sources of their contamination were not known. The EPA, in drilling test wells, soon found TCE and other pollutants in the groundwater near five industrial sites in the area. The two sites owned by large corporations were sensible targets for a lawsuit. These were the old Riley Tannery, belonging to Beatrice Foods, and a machine shop opened in 1960 by the chemical company, W.R. Grace. In 1982 the families of eight leukemia victims (five of them dead) filed a suit, *Anne Anderson et al. v. W.R. Grace & Company and Beatrice Foods, Inc.*, alleging that chemicals from the Beatrice and Grace sites had contaminated Wells G and H, and that prolonged ingestion of these water contaminants had caused the leukemia.

The Trial

The trial took place in U.S. District Court in Boston during 1986 and attracted much attention from the local and national press. Judge

Walter Skinner, anticipating that jurors would hear a lot of technical testimony, separated the trial into phases. In the first phase the jury would decide whether or not Beatrice or Grace had polluted Wells G and H. If they did not, the trial would end. If they did, the jury would take up the medical question: Did the chemicals cause the leukemia?

The six jurors were a utility foreman, a house painter, a postal worker, a retired nurse, a church organist, and a clerk for an insurance company. Witnesses included three hydrologists—one each for the plaintiffs, Beatrice, and Grace—who took hours of testimony to educate the jury about the geology of Woburn and concepts of fluid flow. Afterward one of the jurors, Harriett Clarke, told a conference at Harvard Law School that too much complicated information was presented during seventy-eight days of testimony. "We couldn't absorb day by day what we had. [There was] too much technical stuff for lay people to comprehend" (See http:// cyber.law.harvard.edu/ acivilaction/projover.htm). She said that objections continually interrupted the flow of expert testimony, that there was no way to keep this in your head.

The Beatrice property, comprising the tannery and a fifteen-acre plot where some dumping had occurred, lies on the west side of the Aberjona River, its closest boundary within 200 feet of the wells, which are on the east side of the river. The Grace site is farther away but on the same side of the river as the wells. It was the job of the plaintiffs' and defendants' hydrologic experts, with their mathematical models, to calculate the time it would take chemicals found in the groundwater at both sites to travel though the ground to the wells. Experts for the different sides disagreed on these times.

The plaintiffs' hydrologist used a one-dimensional model of the aquifer to estimate travel time from the Grace site to the wells as three years for TCE, 1.03 years for DCE, and 9.67 years for PCE. His travel times for Beatrice were three months for TCE, 1.03 months for DCE, and 9.67 months for PCE. (It is peculiar that only the units differ between his estimates for Grace and Beatrice.) In his opinion, the chemicals reached Wells G and H from both Grace and Beatrice within the fifteen-year period between 1964 and 1979 when these wells were operational.

The hydrologist hired by Beatrice did not calculate travel times but claimed that when the wells were pumping, water seeping down from the Aberjona River formed a "mound" on the water table, in effect opposing the transverse flow of groundwater under the river. As a result, groundwater on the Beatrice property would flow westward, away from Wells G and H, and therefore could not have contaminated the wells.

Grace's hydrologist, using a three-dimensional model of the aquifer, estimated that in twenty-five years TCE would move less than 1,000 feet from the Grace property toward the wells, and DCE would move less than 1,600 feet. Based on these calculations, he claimed that even if solvents had been released into the groundwater on the day the Grace plant first opened in 1960, they could not have reached Wells G and H, over 2,500 feet away, by 1979 when the wells were shut down.

At the end of testimony, Judge Skinner, in agreement with the attorneys, asked the jury four questions, to be answered for each defendant, based on a preponderance of evidence. I have rephrased them for simplicity.

- Were any of the chemicals—TCE, DCE, or PCE—disposed on the defendant's land, and had these chemicals substantially contaminated the wells before May 22, 1979?

- If yes, what was the earliest date—both the month and year—at which each of these chemicals had substantially contaminated the wells?

- Did this contamination happen because of the defendant's negligence?

- If yes, what was the earliest date—both the month and year—at which the contamination referred to in question three was caused by the negligence of the defendant?

The jurors had been expecting to make a simple determination whether or not the companies were responsible for the contaminated wells. Harriett Clarke said at the Harvard Law School conference, "The first thing we did when we got in the jury room was look at the questions and we laughed—we could either laugh or cry." Mitchell Pacelle, who interviewed five of the six jurors, claims in his article "Contaminated Verdict," published in the *American Lawyer* (December 1986, pp. 75-80), that not one of them understood all the questions. However, the jury's difficulties cannot be blamed wholly on Judge Skinner's requirement that it specify the arrival time of chemicals to the wells because it deadlocked for eight days before taking up that issue.

The bemused jurors immediately split as they tried to answer question one: did Grace or Beatrice dispose of chemicals that contaminated the wells by 1979? Jean Coulsey, whose long-held belief was that "businesses can get away with murder," was in the majority wanting a guilty verdict (Pachelle, p. 78). Harriett Clarke and Robert Fox supported the defendants.

By the afternoon of the second day, the discussion between Fox and Coulsey began to grow heated. The judge had allowed the jurors to take notes during the trial, and Fox had filled the pages of four notebooks. He would read to the other jurors items from his notes that supported his point of view. Coulsey had taken almost no notes. She felt intuitively that the companies were responsible, but she had difficulty articulating her thoughts and could not readily summon facts the way Fox could (Harr, p. 385).

Finally seeing the need for compromise, the jurors agreed to an answer for question one: Grace had contributed to the contamination of the wells, Beatrice had not. With this compromise—in effect absolving Beatrice from blame—the jurors turned to the troubling demand for a specific month and year when Grace contaminated the wells. They quickly agreed that they did not know, writing "not determined" for question two. On the third question they found Grace negligent, essentially keeping the compromise reached on the first question.

The fourth question, similar to question two, also asks for a month and year, but this time it is not the date at which Grace contaminated the wells but the date at which Grace negligently contaminated the wells. Since the jury could not determine the date for question two, it makes no sense to give a specific date for question four. Here the jurors' misunderstanding led them into an error. They came up with a date, September 1973, when Grace had closed a storm drain in which workers had disposed of TCE. Because of this inconsistency, Judge Skinner threw out the verdict and ordered a new trial. Since neither party wanted to repeat the exercise, they reached a settlement with Grace paying $8 million dollars to the plaintiffs but admitting no guilt.

Hydrologic Evidence

Testimony by hydrologic experts was supposed to be central to the case, demonstrating if solvents did or could seep from groundwater on the Beatrice or Grace sites into Wells G and H before the wells were closed in 1979. I will not delve deeply into the complicated and often conflicting statements of the three hydrologists whose 1,800 pages of testimony occupied twenty-one days including seven days just for cross-examination of the plaintiffs' expert. Fortunately Professor E. Scott Bair, a hydrologist at Ohio State University, has examined this in detail, and my treatment depends heavily on his analysis, "Hydrologic Models in the Courtroom" (Department of Geological Sciences, Ohio State University, 2000; also see Bair's website, www.geology.ohio-state.edu/~lahm/).

From Pacelle's and Harr's accounts of the jury's deliberations, and from its answers to Judge Skinner's four questions, it seems that the hydrologic evidence had little bearing on the verdict. Having interviewed five members of the jury, Pacelle writes, "many jurors had judged it all but impossible to believe one expert over another" (p. 78). It is doubtful that the jurors understood the hydrology. Harriett Clarke, in explaining her reasoning in favor of Beatrice, asked how chemicals could have flowed from the Beatrice property through the river, as if she regarded the Aberjona River as blocking chemical migration to the wells, a position that none of the experts had presented.

TCE was found in the groundwater at both sites, at higher concentrations in Beatrice's groundwater than Grace's. But the compromise verdict found only Grace responsible for contaminating the wells, exonerating Beatrice. Apparently this distinction rode on Grace's known use and disposal of TCE on site, thus linking its operations to its groundwater pollution. No one had acknowledged or implicated the Beatrice tannery as a user or disposer of the solvents. (The presence of TCE in Beatrice's groundwater might be explained by illegal dumping on the fifteen-acre plot adjoining the tannery.) But Judge Skinner's first question asks about more than disposal, also inquiring if the pollutants reached the wells by May 22, 1979. This, of course, is the point addressed by the hydrologic models, but apparently the jurors did not address it, in essence ignoring the hydrologic evidence.

It is tempting to blame the jurors' limited education for any deficit in their understanding or use of the hydrology. Perhaps, but Professor Bair, pointing to the month-and-year requirement in questions formulated by the judge and attorneys, suggests that these well educated men also lacked a realistic understanding of hydrologic models, which cannot attain this precision. (Plaintiffs' hydrologist had stated contaminant travel times in hundredths of months, a misuse of significant digits that Bair thinks may have led the judge and attorneys to request an unrealistic degree of precision.) Bair's own post-trial analysis of the hydrology reaches a conclusion nearly opposite to that of the jury: if the wells were contaminated by polluted groundwater from either site, he suggests, it was more likely from Beatrice than Grace.

Splitting the Trial

Judge Skinner had split the trial into compartmentalized phases in order to ease the presentation of technical information. The first phase inquired if the companies had contaminated the wells. If they had not, the trial would end. If they had, the second phase would inquire if the contamination had caused the leukemia. Parents could not testify about their sick children until the second phase of the trial, when illnesses were the issue. The attorneys for Beatrice and Grace were glad of this, knowing that the families would evoke sympathy from the jury. Jan Schlichtmann, lead attorney for the plaintiffs (and protagonist of *A Civil Action*), did not care one way or the other, but his associate on the case, Professor Charles Nesson of Harvard Law School, thought the split trial a disadvantage to the plaintiffs (Harr, p. 287).

After the trial, students in Professor Nesson's evidence class developed a clever experiment to explore whether or not the split produced a different verdict than might have been reached if the water argument had been presented in a unified way. The class prepared a unified argument for each side (also adding information that was not available at the original trial); its evidentiary points were shown in order of presentation. The class then used the same evidence to prepare a split argument in which points focused on contamination were presented in phase one (left column) and points focused on leukemia were presented in phase two (right column).

Both conditions—unified and split—were fleshed out and mounted on a separate website (cyber.law.harvard.edu/evidence99/woburn/intro.html). The two conditions showed nearly identical web pages. Using a quasi-random procedure, subjects were assigned to the unified or split condition. (By March 2000 there were 405 subjects in the unified condition and 300 in the split condition, an uneven distribution that suggests assignment was not random.) Those viewing the unified argument were asked at the end if Grace caused leukemia in Woburn. Those viewing the split argument were asked, after phase one, if Grace had polluted Wells G and H. For those voting no, the trial ended. Those voting yes went on to the second phase and at the end were asked if Wells G and H caused leukemia in Woburn.

The result: In the unified condition, 72 percent of subjects voted that Grace caused leukemia in Woburn. In the split condition, only 35 percent of subjects voted that Grace polluted the wells and that the wells caused leukemia. Thus, Professor Nesson's class supported his contention that plaintiffs were disadvantaged by the split trial.

However the reasons for this remain unclear. I doubt that one condition evoked a stronger emotional response than the other did because both appear aseptic on the web. (No pictures are shown of grieving parents or sickly children.) Possibly uncertainties in the evidence are more apparent when it is presented in the smaller doses of the split format, which would benefit the defendant. Another possibility is that it was the format of voting, rather than the format of the argument, that affected the outcome. Subjects in the split condition had to vote twice to reach a "guilty" verdict, subjects in the unified condition voted only once. Seventy-five percent of subjects in the split condition blamed Grace for the polluted wells, half of these blamed the wells for the leukemia. If subjects in the unified condition had been asked to cast the same two votes, they might have given similar responses. Unfortunately these possibilities were not pursued in the experiment.

If we take the experiment at face value, it appears that subjects' verdicts depend as much on whether the argument is split or unified as on the substantive content of the evidence. This is a disheartening result for those who look to lay juries for a rational evaluation of scientific data, though for all we know a jury of experts would be similarly swayed by the format of presentation.

Uses and Misuses of Science in the Law

"Woburn remains a principal training ground for lawyers on both sides of the toxic tort litigation field on the difficulties inherent in full blown adjudication, to a lay jury, of cases based on complicated, and controversial, scientific evidence.... As much money as the Woburn plaintiffs spent, and as well as they did comparatively, no one involved in the lawsuit is likely to describe the outcome as making anyone whole" (Robert Condlin, "What's Really Going On?" *Rutgers Computer and Technology Law Journal* 25 (1999), p. 211).

It would be a useful exercise to compare the Woburn trial with trials that have used science to better effect. Then, perhaps, we could identify procedures that either aid or inhibit juries in reaching verdicts consistent with a competent reading of technical evidence. We might find, for example, that in the successful trials, expert testimony is relatively free of interruption by opposing attorneys, or that it is concise rather than drawn out over days.

Possibly we would find that none of this makes much difference—that complex scientific testimony is intrinsically difficult for a lay jury to absorb—in which case other options should be considered. Perhaps technical experts, rather than testifying individually, could present their material in the format of a seminar mediated by a court-appointed master. The goal of this seminar would be to solicit from the experts a list of relevant scientific points upon which they agreed, and also a list of relevant scientific points upon which they disagreed. If all parties agreed to these lists, they could be presented to the jury in a straightforward manner, concisely and relatively free of objections, to serve as the scientific basis for a verdict.

Part 2

Searching for Science Policy

5

The Use and Abuse of Science in Drug Abuse Control Policy

Mark A. R. Kleiman

As with any sacred term, "science" is irreducibly ambiguous, and its ambiguities create confusion around its appropriate use in policymaking. There is widespread agreement that drug policy ought to be made on a scientific basis, but that verbal agreement masks at least two quite different intentions.

It would be hard to argue against the proposition that policy-making ought to be informed by what Russell called "the scientific temperament," defined as "giving to every proposition that degree of assent warranted by evidence and argument."[1] In that sense, there is a strong argument that a good dose of "science" is exactly what drug policy needs.

But "science" also names a particular set of social enterprises, marked by the competitive pursuit of interesting new systematic knowledge of physical, biological, and social phenomena. The claim of these enterprises to dominance in policymaking, about drugs or many other topics is much weaker than might appear at first blush.

No one doubts that science in this second sense has a great deal to contribute to policymaking, in the form of (1) predictive knowledge about what is likely to happen, (2) contingently predictive knowledge about the likely consequences of different actions, and (3) technological knowledge about means to accomplishing chosen ends. But that "science," so understood, ought to dominate policy-making is much less clear. It has its own goals and purposes, and its participants have their own career strategies, which may be at odds with the needs of policymaking.

Moreover, any intellectual enterprise that influences high-stakes social processes will attract attempts will be made to influence its results for extrinsic reasons, and by means contrary to its internal logic. That is no less true of science today than of theology in the ages of faith.

This essay explores the multiple gaps between the scientific enterprise as actually practiced by working scientists, their host institutions, and their funding bodies, and as then disseminated to the public and used in the processes of political decision-making, and the requirements of a hypothetical process of rational or policy-analytic ("scientific" in the broader sense) policy choice, with specific reference to drug policy.

Both the standards of what constitutes important science, and the experimental method of trying to isolate the effects of on variable at a time, are often at odds with the needs of policymaking.

With respect to standards: Some crucial bits of knowledge, as evaluated from the policy analyst's viewpoint, may not be interesting, new, or systematic as evaluated from the viewpoint of a working scientist. If a particular piece of research doesn't count as important science to others in the field, the rewards in scientific-career terms from taking it on will be slight, no matter how great its potential value to a hypothetical rational social decision-maker.

A prominent, though perhaps not important, example, is the question of the medical uses of cannabis. Delta-9 THC, the primary psychoactive agent in the cannabis plant, having already been approved for medical use, the remaining question from a drug-regulation standpoint is whether the inhaled vapors of the whole plant, containing a mix of psychoactive agents, might outperform the oral administration of the pure delta-9. Both anecdote and theory suggest that this might be true (patients taking pure delta-9 tend to complain of an unpleasantly anxious intoxication, and delta-9 has been shown to have anxiety-inducing effects, while cannabidiol, one of the other active agents, has been shown to be anxiety-reducing[2]; moreover, inhalation has advantages over pill-swallowing in both speed and the capacity for the patient to adjust the dose), but the superiority of whole plant vapor over the THC pill has yet to be shown in controlled trials.[3]

There has been lots of huffing and puffing over the medical marijuana issue, including several state-level referenda, years of federal court litigation, and an Institute of Medicine report, but no one has done the simple experiment of giving the two alternative drug/dosage forms to a group of patients and finding out what happens.

Part of the reason, to be sure, is deliberate obstructionism on the part of the National Institute on Drug Abuse, which has both a strong ideological position against the use of whole cannabis (rather than particular molecules) as medicine and a monopoly on research supplies of the drug. But there has been no flood of research applications, and NIDA has had no difficulty in finding a "lack of scientific merit" in those that have been submitted. The question of whether the vapors from a whole plant are better or worse, in terms of a side-effect not subject to direct measurement, than the oral administration of one of its components is simply not a scientifically interesting question, especially when the answer is not really in doubt given the previous research with the two components. As a result, opponents of the medical use of the whole plant can continue to say, accurately though disingenuously, that its superiority to pure delta-9 "has not been scientifically established."[4]

With respect to experimental technique: an experimentalist tries to manipulate phenomena so that only one independent variable changes at a time; that's what a controlled experiment is about. But the world policymakers must live in is not so neat; the effect of maternal cocaine use on fetal development, controlling for maternal alcohol use, is no doubt an interesting topic in pharmacology, but since in fact cocaine consumption tends to increase alcohol consumption, the finding that cocaine itself is only modestly damaging to the fetus may be seriously misleading, given how much damage is done by the accompanying alcohol. (And, as Harold Pollack has pointed out, most of the damage to the child may come through the impact of its mother's continued drug abuse on her nurturing behavior, rather than through any effect of prenatal exposure.)[5]

Conflict between good and interesting science and the needs of policy-making is more typical than anomalous. Consider four fairly standard questions in drug policy—not in the debate over drug policy in the large ("the drug war" v. "drug policy reform," or "prohibition" v. "legalization") that dominates media attention to this subject without having much impact on actual governmental behavior, but in day-to-day decision-making about drugs:

1. Should we raise the tax on a standard alcoholic drink, currently about a dime, to some substantially higher number, say twenty cents?

2. Should we reduce the number of cocaine dealers in prison by 20%, using some combination of reduced police activity, less vigorous prosecution, and changes in sentencing laws? (Or should we instead do nothing, or raise that number by 20 %?)

3. Should we increase public funding for methadone maintenance therapy enough to raise the number of methadone clients at any one time by one-quarter? How about outpatient drug-free therapy for those suffering from substance abuse disorders relating to cocaine or methamphetamine?

4. Should schools devote an additional hour per week of class time to delivering anti-drug messages?

What science would be helpful in making these decisions correctly? Put another way, what parameters would it be useful to measure before choosing?

Issue 1: Alcohol Taxation

Consider first how the policy works, for good and for ill. Higher taxes will raise prices; higher prices will lead to lower consumption of alcohol and its complements (very likely including cocaine and the amphetamines) and higher consumption of its substitutes (heroin, possibly cannabis, certainly alcohol treatment).

Reducing drinking will tend, other things equal, to reduce drinking-related problems, both physical and behavioral, including the rate of addiction. Increasing the price of drinking, however, will tend to impoverish those who remain heavy drinkers in the face of the tax increase, with bad effects on them and possibly on their neighbors. It will also cause some persons whose drinking was a harmless pleasure to cut back or even stop, reducing their well-being and in some cases even damaging their health somewhat.

Thinking as policymakers, we are interested in the absolute and relative magnitudes of these changes. If the gains from reduced problem drinking, including complements and net of substitutes, outweigh the losses from displaced harmless drinking plus the impoverishment effect on poor heavy drinkers, the tax increase should be adopted; else not.

A partial list of facts relevant to this simple decision that are, (at least in principle) scientifically determinable would therefore include:

- Price-elasticity of demand for alcohol, disaggregated by user characteristics (age, drinking intensity, preferred form of alcohol, behavior while drunk), and into effects on initiation, continuation, intensification, quit, and relapse rates for casual and problematic alcohol use.

- The relationships of substitution or complementarity (technically, the cross-elasticities of demand) between alcohol and other drugs.

- The impact on future drinking of price-induced changes in current drinking by minors.

- Dose-effect curves for physical toxicity (liver, heart, etc.) disaggregated by user characteristics.

- Dose-effect curves for behavioral toxicity (crime, accident, suicide, degradation of workplace and family performance), similarly disaggregated.

- Lost well-being (measured in the economist's "willingness-to-pay" measure) suffered by drinkers and their intimates from becoming addicted to alcohol (on some definition of "addicted") and of the gains from any given period of recovery.

- The impact on welfare and behavior of heavy drinkers who continue to drink heavily in the face of the tax-induced price increase.

Notice that the hot scientific topics (receptors, genetic predispositions, "rational addiction," etc.) have little or nothing to offer here. Notice also that the listed questions have mostly unknown answers. And yet the topic is arguably the most practically important in all of drug policy, since it concerns the drug that does more damage to users and others than all the rest combined and a policy that is virtually self-implementing.

Issue 2: Changing the Number of Cocaine Dealers in Prison

An analysis of the impact of changing the number of cocaine dealers in prison calls for much the same analysis, except that the effects on price (and non-price factors of availability), which we could assume as known in the alcohol-tax case, are in fact almost entirely speculative, and may depend a great deal on who goes to prison rather than the mere number of prisoners. But the basic logic of making a damaging drug more expensive or harder to get is the same: the key questions are how much a given change will reduce consumption, and how much that reduction in consumption will in turn reduce harms to users and others. To the damage on the user side, we have to add both the costs and suffering due to imprisonment (net of its benefits in preventing non-drug crime by those imprisoned) and possible bad effects on the dealer side: making cocaine more expensive can raise the revenues in the illicit market and thus the rewards of successful dealing.

Once again, knowing more about the reward pathways in the nucleus accumbens isn't likely to offer much guidance, and almost no research is completed or underway that would provide convincing quantitative answers to the questions that do matter. (The crude fact that the price of cocaine has fallen by about three-quarters in the face of a decade and a half of greatly stepped-up enforcement provides a strong hint about one key answer, but there is no published attempt to estimate the impact of an extra dealer-year of imprisonment on the price of cocaine.) Here again, the topic is of overwhelming importance; we have something like a third of a million cocaine dealers behind bars at any moment, costing a fortune (or, to think about it a different way, using up many prison cells that could otherwise be holding muggers) and suffering greatly. If, in fact, reducing that number substantially wouldn't greatly increase cocaine consumption, there's an opportunity for huge gains in fiscal, crime-control, and humanitarian terms. But our scientists don't seem to be much help in making this choice wisely.

As Peter Reuter has eloquently pointed out, the drug research budget is very tightly concentrated on biomedicine, prevention, and treatment, while the drug abuse control budget is overwhelmingly devoted to enforcement.[6] This means that even the most basic relationships between enforcement effort and drug-abuse (or even drug-market) outcomes remain almost entirely matters of speculation. Since this situation is not disadvantageous to the powerful political and bureaucratic interests associated with law enforcement (it is well known that evaluating a program is one of the best ways to kill it), it is unlikely to change. But unless it does change, we will have neither any way of knowing whether enforcement does any good, and if so, what kind of enforcement does what kind of good, nor any way of optimizing the use of a given set of enforcement resources over a set of social objectives.

Issue 3: Public Policy and Drug Treatment

In order to address this issue, we would need to know how much damage is currently being done to and by those persons not now in one or another kind of drug treatment who would be in such treatment if the supply were expanded, and how much less damage would occur if they were treatment clients instead of untreated illicit drug consumers. This is not a question that the standard "treatment effectiveness" studies are much use in answering. A substantial amount is known about the differences in behavior between treatment clients before and after their treatment entry, but using the difference as an estimate of the benefit of the treatment is highly problematic, since it requires that we ignore both self-selection and regression toward the mean. Nor would a random-assignment experiment tell us much about a world in which potential clients search for programs (and vice versa). Conceptually, the right experiment would be an intervention randomly assigning members of some population not to different treatments, but to different levels of treatment availability (e.g., by handing half the group coupons guaranteeing no-wait treatment, the other half not).

Issue 4: School-Based Drug Abuse Prevention Programs

As to the question of whether school-based prevention efforts should be expanded, curtailed or substantially modified, the answer surely depends in part on the content of the classroom message and the competence with which it is delivered. The (rather depressing) prevention-evaluation literature has a great deal to say about the former, but tells us much less about the importance of the latter. Since an actual school district cannot count on having its actual teachers deliver anti-drug messages with the zeal or skill of those who run pilot programs, evaluation results are likely to be systematically over-optimistic.[7]

But the deeper problem here involves time. What we really want to know is the effect of the program on the long-term risk of developing clinically significant substance abuse problems. But only a small proportion of seventh-graders will become drug addicts, and even they will not do so for several to many years. Even if someone were willing to fund the enormous sample sizes and long-term follow-ups required to learn about the efficacy of a program measured in these terms, the result would come so many years later than the intervention that its applicability to then-current conditions would be open to serious question. So instead we measure the impact of the programs on initiation rates to tobacco, alcohol, and cannabis, trusting that the correlation between early use and later problems is causal rather than deriving from unmeasured characteristics of the children involved.

This is no mere methodological quibble. One of the best-established scientific findings about drug abuse prevention is that "information only" prevention programs are counterproductive, because they increase the rate of experimentation by making children feel that they are sophisticated drug consumers. That finding led to the development of later prevention models, based on social influence. But an information-based program could, in principle, increase the rate of initiation but more-than-offsettingly reduce the risk of getting into trouble conditional on initiation. So far all we know the discredited programs were in fact succeeding in reducing the risk that their subjects would develop clinical substance abuse disorder.

In this case, there is no need to go beyond the range of what is scientifically determinable to answer the policy-relevant question. It's simply that the science involved would be too expensive and time-consuming.

The Limits of Science

In sum, then, doing more and better science of the kind we currently do wouldn't give us much in the way of usable answers to these four rather typical drug-policy problems, even if anyone wanted the answers.

There are often unavoidable tensions between scientific interest and short-term practical utility: on this score, there is not much difference between drug abuse research and mental health research, where the families of those with severe Axis I disorders such as schizophrenia want work on treating those diagnoses, while the scientists want to learn how the brain works. Research funders with a strong desire for the right answers to practically important questions can ensure that pure scientific merit is not the only thing scientists consider in choosing research topics. (And, needless to say, there are plenty of scientists whose own commitment to curing disease or solving social problems leads them to work voluntarily on less scientifically interesting questions.)

There are also unavoidable tensions between both the caution and the boldness of scientists (boldness in conjecture, caution about drawing firm conclusions) and the needs of legal and bureaucratic decision-makers for "hard evidence" or "scientific proof" to support decisions, especially those that go against prevailing modes of thought. Popper's principle that scientific theories do not become "more probable" in the sense of the probability calculus as evidence mounts in their favor (because the truth is of measure zero in the mass of possible conjecture) means that the best-supported hypothesis, the one on the basis of which one can most productively conduct research, may not be the same as a reasonable Bayesian prior about some set of real-world relationships.

On top of the inevitable problems, there are also (theoretically) avoidable problems, which resemble nothing so much as the "idols" Bacon saw as interfering with the proper scientific interpretation of nature. We can classify them roughly as idols of the newspaper, idols of the enterprise, and idols of the laboratory. The case of substance abuse encounters them in an especially rich set of ways, but every field has such idols.

The Idols of the Newspaper

The idols of the newspaper are the received truths, "known" to every reporter and newspaper-reader, but false-to-fact. To deny any of them is to discredit oneself.

For example, any use of any illicit drug is officially believed to carry a high risk of developing into problem use. In fact, however, the most common use pattern for the most common psychoactive substances (except for nicotine in the form of cigarettes) is occasional and non-problematic.[8] The lifetime probability of developing diagnosable substance abuse disorder, conditional on a non-trivial initiation to cannabis, powder cocaine, or alcohol, seems to run between 10% and 25%, with alcohol on the high end of that range, perhaps because of its ubiquity, and cannabis at the low end.[9]

Moreover, substance abuse disorders are "known" to be chronic and relapsing and to rarely go into remission without professional help or participation in structured group self-help. In fact, the most common pattern of substance abuse disorder has a relatively rapid remission (several months to a few years) with no relapse, and the vast majority of those who have had, but no longer actively suffer from, diagnosable substance abuse disorder have had no formal treatment: they just quit when they got tired.[10]

Those who cannot quit on their own and need formal treatment are indeed much more likely to have stubborn problems—use of tobacco cessation services is negatively correlated with the probability of successful quitting—but even among those who enter treatment, only a minority keeps cycling in and out. However, this group accounts for a large proportion of those in treatment at any given time, and is therefore taken by treatment professionals to represent the typical pattern.

The drug problem is "known" to consist primarily of illicit drug use; in fact, about 85% of all diagnosable substance abuse disorder (again, leaving the non-intoxicant nicotine aside) involves alcohol as the primary or sole substance. Yet the newspapers routinely report that so-and-so drinks but "does not use drugs."

Similarly, everyone "knows" that babies exposed to cocaine in utero (the famous "crack babies") are irreparably damaged. In fact, the dimensions of such damage have not been established, and there is reason to think that bad parenting due to continued maternal substance abuse has more to do with bad outcomes than prenatal exposure.[11] It is certainly the case that total fetal damage from maternal use of alcohol, and total fetal damage from maternal use of tobacco (which is known to reduce measured IQ by about a third of a standard deviation) each dwarfs the damage from cocaine.[12]

Anyone who pays scientific attention to the drug problem knows that these idols of the newspaper have feet of clay. Their persistence is due in part to their serviceability in the drug-prevention field as bogey-men with which to frighten children. The lack of a cadre of experienced, full-time drug reporters comparable to the reporters who have made careers covering national defense or the environment also helps to maintain these idols on their pedestals; the average reporter assigned to a drug story doesn't know any more about the underlying phenomenon than her readers, or for that matter her editors. Iconoclasm is both dangerous in career terms and unlikely to make any headway against reporters' ignorance and editors' sense that they ought not to be interfering with the national anti-drug-abuse campaign by printing inconvenient facts that most readers wouldn't believe anyway.

The Idols of the Enterprise

The idols of the enterprise are organizational self-interests, whether embodied in public agencies or private industries, that would be damaged by the recognition of certain facts.

Twice in the past fifteen years, agencies engaged in drug interdiction have hired tame research organizations to produce pseudo-scientific findings showing that the interdiction effort is highly valuable. Demonstrating the fallacies involved requires no analytic tools past first-year microeconomics. Yet, under Congressional pressure the Office of National Drug Control Policy funded, and the National Academy of Sciences conducted, a solemn review in which one of these spoof documents was treated on an equal footing with a serious, though admittedly preliminary, piece of analysis arguing for the superiority of treatment over enforcement; both were even-handedly condemned as imperfect and therefore inadequate as bases for policy-making.[13]

That the National Institute on Drug Abuse has a drug-abuse-prevention brief as well as a research brief imports idols of the agency into the process by which drug-related science is funded and its results disseminated. If there has even been a NIDA press release about the finding that some illicit drug does *not* in fact have some hypothesized danger, no one seems to have reported it. A recent study of dance-club drug-taking in Europe compared a group of extremely heavy Ecstasy users (Ecstasy is nominally MDMA, but there is evidence of substantial adulteration and mislabeling, in addition to substantial deliberate polydrug abuse among the sample) with two control groups: very heavy cannabis users, and those not using any drug heavily. It was not surprising that the official NIDA line, dutifully reported in the mass media, was that the study showed MDMA to be a terribly dangerous drug, even though the actual measured impacts were rather slight given the truly heroic dosing patterns involved and despite the doubts about how much of the damage was actually from MDMA.[14] It took more gall, though not more than the NIDA Director proved to be master of, to simply ignore the finding that the (extremely) heavy cannabis users were not measurably different from the other control group on any dimension of damage. That finding, though reported clearly albeit unmethodically in the actual research paper, disappeared down the journalistic memory hole.

On the licit-drug side of the problem, both the alcohol and the tobacco industries have created pseudo-disputes over whether their products are "drugs." (One of the trade associations on the alcohol side offers the thought that because alcohol is used in grams-per-kilogram rather than milligrams-per-kilogram doses, it isn't really a drug. No, I'm not making this up.)

Idols of the Laboratory

Idols of the laboratory are principles for conducting and interpreting research that get in the way of the search for truth. Some are imposed from outside; others are chosen for various reasons by the research communities themselves.

Start with the external problems. Whenever "science" is invested with legal or other political significance, interested parties will have reasons to try to cheat by influencing results, using some combination of funding, pressure, and outright lying. The result is often the creation of extra-scientific methodological rules intended to make cheating harder, leading to a process that might be called "forensic science" to distinguish it from the genuine article. Benefit/cost analysis, studies of environmental impacts and remediation, and the evaluation of proposed new pharmaceutical drugs all proceed under the rules of forensic science. Typical "rules of the game" in such circumstances require ignoring any data not from a limited range of study types and treating effects that cannot be estimated with precision as if they were known to be zero.

Perhaps the most sacred of such idols of the (forensic) laboratory is the double-blind placebo-controlled experiment. As a method, it builds in maximum protections against investigator deception and self-deception. But in the case of the psychoactive drugs, it can lead to either the impossibility of doing any experiment or to the performance of an experiment that misses the point. Keeping the subject "blind" to whether his or her neurons are being bombarded is often tricky, though the use of an "active placebo" can help. In cases where the intervention involves human interaction between therapist and patient rather than the mere administration of a chemical, it can be difficult or impossible to keep a competent clinician in the dark as to whether the patient has had an active dose or not. Even where possible, a double-blind study introduces an element of unrealism into the results, since in actual clinical practice patients and physicians do know what they're getting and giving. None of this is to say that double-blind trials aren't worth doing. But to insist that *only* such trials are potential sources of scientific knowledge is surely idolatry.

Human-subjects protection rules can also function as extrinsic idols of the laboratory. Imposed on scientists after some fairly horrendous abuses, their implementation thorough Institutional Review Boards (and in the special case of California, through something called, improbably, the California Research Advisory Panel) can serve as a convenient way of side-tracking research likely to lead to inconvenient results, especially when the potential benefits to subjects are ruled out of consideration because the subjects are not suffering from any disease and therefore cannot by definition experience clinical benefit. The fact that some of the potential subjects will instead take the same drugs (or what they fondly imagine to be the same drugs) illicitly and therefore under uncontrolled conditions does not constitute a counter-argument, as the Institutional Review Board game is played.

A drug-specific idol of the laboratory is the convention, respected by funders and journals alike, that the sheerest anecdotal (i.e., case-report) or correlational data should be accepted as science if it seems to show that some drug does damage, but that only carefully controlled studies suffice to show benefit. This is related, but not identical, to the notion, enshrined in FDA practice though not in statute, that the only legitimate use of a drug (psychoactive or not) is to treat some diagnosable pathology, and that improvements in normal functioning do not constitute "efficacy." (The practice of "off-label" prescribing allows many drugs approved for treatment of genuine disease to then be used widely for performance enhancement, as the case of Viagra graphically demonstrates, but without the existence of a clinical entity called erectile dysfunction the mere desire of middle-aged men to perform better sexually would not have justified a drug approval. One might reasonably ask, "Why not?")

Other idols of the laboratory have to do with the needs of normal science to produce papers and for funders to find projects to pay for. The theory of "rational addiction" is a case in point.[15] It turns out that, with appropriate assumptions, some of the phenomena of addiction (such as sudden cessation) can be reproduced within the framework of the rational-actor model beloved of economists.[16] The correspondence to real phenomena is not really very impressive; in particular, if addiction were truly a rational phenomenon, it wouldn't be much of a problem except for its external costs. But the theory allows the production of an almost unlimited number of well-crafted empirical papers, testing the theory against various data sets. As a result, rational addiction has established itself as a major subfield within addiction studies, heavily funded by the National Institute on Alcohol Abuse and Alcoholism and done largely under the highly respectable auspices of the National Bureau of Economic Research.

The great idol of the statistical laboratory is the preference for precision, and especially precision in the measurement of errors of estimate, over relevance to phenomena or to policy. The two hugely expensive national annual surveys on drug abuse, one of households and the other of high-school students, are conducted according to the most rigorous standards of statistical practice. But neither was designed to provide a representative sample at the level of particular states. As a result, they cannot be used to study the impact of variations in state policies on outcomes. Or rather, they could not be used without introducing errors into the standard errors of estimate; as a result, the convention within the field is that these two data sets are not to be used in that way. (Another laboratory idol, confidentiality protection, has been used by one of the survey operators to ensure that such "inappropriate" studies simply cannot be done, because the data for them will not be made available.)

What most striking about all this precision is how easily it lives with gross and palpable inaccuracy. The household survey has a "refused/not home" rate of about 20%, not a very high number but a huge problem when studying behaviors with single-digit prevalences. Moreover, by its design it excludes the homeless and institutional populations, known to contain concentrations of persons with severe substance abuse disorders. As a result, the survey omits about 80% of heavy cocaine users and about 90% of total cocaine consumption. Yet its results, with precisely estimated error bands specifying the likely effects of random sampling error (while ignoring, per convention, the much larger but quantitatively uncertain effects of systematic error) continue to be solemnly published each year, and learned papers continue to cite its findings and use the resulting data set to estimate various equations. After all, it's a well-maintained data set, with a known sampling frame and well-specified standard errors of estimate.

By contrast, the low-budget system that measures drug abuse among arrestees, a system that detects about three-quarters of the heavy cocaine users, is that utterly despicable entity, "a mere convenience sample." Its lack of a true sampling frame disqualifies it from scientific respectability, just as the lack of an adequate number of quarterings of nobility disqualified bourgeois candidates from French military commissions under the ancient regime. After all, one must maintain *some* standards.

Conclusion

There are both intrinsic and extrinsic reasons why "science" proper has less to contribute to making better drug abuse control policies than might be thought. But the scientific temperament—the obstinate insistence on knowing what one knows and what one doesn't know, and making the best decisions possible with the data in hand —remains our best hope for digging ourselves out of the ditch in which our current grossly unscientific policies have landed us.

Notes

1. See, for example, Russell, Bertrand (1962) *The Scientific Outlook.* New York, New York: W.W. Norton & Company.
2. Zuardi, A.W., et al (1982). "Action of Cannabidiol on the Anxiety and Other Effects Produced by Delta-9-THC in Normal Subjects," *Psychopharmacology* 76:245-250.
3. Institute of Medicine (1999). *Marijuana and Medicine.* Washington, D.C. : National Academy Press
4. Drug Enforcement Administration (1994). *Drug Legalization: Myths and Misconceptions Washington,* D.C.: U.S. Department of Justice.
5. Pollack, Harold "When Pregnant Women Use Crack," *Drug Policy Analysis Bulletin* # 8, February 2000.
6. Reuter, Peter (1997). "Hawks Ascendant: The Punitive Trend of American Drug Policy." In: McShane, Marilyn & Williams, Frank P., III, Eds., *Drug Use and Drug Policy.* New York: Garland. See also National Research Council (2001). *Informing America's Policy on Illegal Drugs: What We Don't Know Keeps Hurting Us* Washington, D.C.: National Academy Press.
7. Caulkins, J., Rydell, C.P., Everingham, S., et al. (1999). *An Ounce of Prevention, A Pound of Uncertainty: The Cost-Effectiveness of School-Based Drug Prevention Programs.* Santa Monica, CA: RAND.
8. Reuter, Peter (1999) "Drug Use Measures: What Are They Really Telling Us" *National Institute of Justice Journal* April 1999 pp 12-19.
9. Perrine, D. M. (1996). *The Chemistry of Mind-Altering Drugs — History, Pharmacology, and Cultural Context.* Washington, D.C.: American Chemical Society
10. Heyman, Gene M. "Is Addiction a Chronic, Relapsing Disease?" in Heymann, Phillip B. & Brownsberger, William N. (2001) *Drug Addiction and Drug Policy: The Struggle to Control Dependence.* Cambridge, Massachusetts: Harvard University Press.
11. Pollack, H. "When Pregnant Women Use Crack."
12. Fried, P., Watkinson, B. and Gray, R. (1998) "Differential Effects on Cognitive Functioning in 9- to 12-Year-Olds Prenatally Exposed to Cigarettes and Marihuana," *Neurotoxicology and Teratology, Vol. 20,* No. 3, 1998, pp. 293-306. And: Olds D, Henderson C Jr., Tatelbaum R. (1994) "Intellectual Impairment in Children of Women who Smoke Cigarettes During Pregnancy." *Pediatrics* 1994; 93(2):221-7.
13. Manski, Charles F., Pepper, John V., and Thomas, Yonette F., (Editors) (1999). *Assessment of Two Cost-Effectiveness Studies on Cocaine Control Policy.* Washington, D.C.: National Academy Press – See also Rydell, C. Peter Susan S. Everingham (1994) *Controlling Cocaine: Supply Versus Demand .* Santa Monica, California: RAND Publications – and Caulkins, J. P., Chiesa, J.R., and Everingham, S. (2000) *Response to NRC Assessment of RAND's "Controlling Cocaine" Study.* Santa Monica, CA: RAND Publications.
14. Bolla, K.I. et al (1998) "Memory Impairment in Abstinent MDMA ("Ecstasy") Users." *Neurology.* 1998;51: 1532-1537.

15. Becker, G.S and Murphy, K.M (1988). "A Theory of Rational Addiction." *Journal of Political Economy.* 96:4.
16. Chaloupka, Frank J. "Rational Addictive Behavior and Cigarette Smoking." *Journal of Political Economy.* 1991, May. 99(4): 722-742.

6

Social Science Findings and the "Family Wars"

Norval Glenn

Virtually every aspect of the complex relationship between social science and ideology is prominently present in the heated debates about family issues in the United States and other modern societies. The debates, which center around differential evaluation of such recent family changes as the increase in one-parent families, have become so heated that they are frequently called, with only moderate hyperbole, the "family wars." Family issues have become politicized to an unprecedented extent, with various kinds of liberals, conservatives, and centrists engaging in political action to further their values and beliefs about families. Almost all participants in the debates cite social scientific findings to support their positions, sometimes appropriately and sometimes not. Although there have been numerous biased and unscientific uses of social science evidence in the debates, constructive contributions of social science have been common. For example, several prominent social scientists have let their research lead them to conclusions unpopular among their peers, different from ones they had earlier embraced, and probably contrary to what they would like to conclude.

In this chapter, I first give my view of the relationship between social science and ideological debates, arguing that involvement of social scientists is inevitable and can be appropriate and constructive. I then give examples of both constructive and inappropriate uses of social scientific findings in the family wars, which I use as a basis for suggestions in the final section about how constructive uses can be maximized and misuses minimized.

Social Science and Ideological Debates

Views of how social science should relate to ideology vary between two extremes, namely (a) that social science should be "value free" and thus should remain aloof from ideological conflicts, and (b) that social science should be an instrument for social change and thus should promote the "correct" values and ideological positions. I argue that neither extreme view can be justified, for reasons that can be explained only after an examination of the nature of ideology.

Ideology consists of sets of interrelated (a) beliefs about the nature of reality and (b) values, or beliefs about what is good and what is bad, what is desirable and what is undesirable. In turn, there are two kinds of values, *ultimate* and *derivative*.[1] Ultimate values depend in no direct and readily apparent way on beliefs about the nature of empirical reality. When one is asked why one holds such a value, one does not make a statement of empirical fact to justify it, such as that whatever is valued is good because it has a particular effect. Rather, one will say something on the order of "it is good just because it is" or "because God wills it." If a statement about reality is made to justify an ultimate value, it will be about a transcendent, nonempirical reality rather than one amenable to scientific investigation. Examples of ultimate values for most people who hold them are beliefs that happiness is better than unhappiness and that life is better than death. In contrast, what I call a derivative value depends upon—is *derived* from—both an ultimate value and a belief about the nature of empirical reality, as when someone says that marital stability is good because it contributes to the well-being of children. In other words, a derivative value is linked to an ultimate value by a belief about the nature of nontranscendent reality. The same value may be ultimate to one person and derivative to another. For instance, some people believe divorce is bad because they think it is contrary to the Will of God, while others believe it is undesirable only because they think it typically or often has certain negative consequences for one or more of their ultimate values.

In practice, it is not always possible to make a clear distinction between ultimate and derivative values. For instance, the debate about abortion might seem to be one of the purest examples of a clash of ultimate values, reflecting differences, based in religion and metaphysical assumptions, on the value placed on prenatal human life.

However, new findings about the ability of late-term fetuses to think and feel may well affect the extent to which one values prenatal life. Furthermore, as I point out below, there is a widespread tendency for derivative values to become ultimate ones.

Nevertheless, the conceptual distinction between ultimate and derivative values is useful, there being a class of values that are largely, if not entirely, immune to scientific assessment. This does not mean, however, that these values are not relevant to social science. Were there not widespread adherence to certain ultimate values concerning the human condition, there would be no public support for social science. And although some social scientists may be motivated solely by intellectual curiosity, it is likely that most entered the field in hopes of furthering their ultimate values. Of course, the view that knowledge is better than ignorance is an ultimate value for some people who hold it.

More important for my task here is the fact that social science can assess the validity of the beliefs about reality that link derivative to ultimate values. The family wars, in common with most ideological debates, are to a large extent, an interplay of competing derivative values. There is much more agreement on ultimate values and goals than on how different family arrangements, and the social policies that affect those arrangements, promote or inhibit attainment of those goals. In other words, the family wars are to a large extent about empirical matters—the subject matter of family social science. Given this fact, family social scientists cannot avoid involvement in ideological and political debates; whatever they conclude on the basis of their research and theorizing will be used by participants in the debates, whether the social scientists want that to happen or not. It is hard to imagine how family social scientists could keep their work so abstract, or so trivial, that it would have little or no relevance to current debates on family issues.

This characterization of the part social science can and should play in ideological conflicts makes the fundamental rule to be followed by social scientists, and by those who use social scientific evidence, quite simple. These persons need only to (a) remain true to their ultimate values while (b) avoiding dogmatic adherence to derivative values, the latter being a necessary condition for the former. Although this admonition is simple, following it is not, because several major influences tend to prevent adherence to it.

One of the most important of these is the tendency for activists and researchers to become so publicly associated with derivative values that they become ego involved in the defense of those values. For example, an author who has argued forcefully that family structure makes little difference for child outcomes may continue to defend that position even in the face of strong evidence that it is incorrect. In other words, derivative values may become transformed into ultimate ones; what was once a means to an end may become an end in itself. Admission that adherence to a derivative value has been based on an incorrect assessment of reality is likely to be especially difficult for activists; to do so would often entail their facing up to the futility, or even the destructiveness, of what they have been doing.

Another major influence that tends to hamper the accurate assessment of the empirical allegations that support derivative values is the need of activists and researchers to gain the approval of their "significant others"—those whose views of them matter. This need can be a strong deterrent to reporting, or even believing, unpopular conclusions, regardless of the strength of the supporting evidence. For activists concerned with family issues, the nature of bias from this source varies widely, depending on the organizations and ideological factions to which they belong. For family social scientists, the bias is almost uniformly in a liberal direction, that is, toward positive or sanguine evaluations of the effects of recent family trends.

Yet another complication for the assessment of derivative values is the fact that a derivative value may relate to more than one ultimate value, and relate to them in contradictory ways. Suppose, for instance, that the object of a derivative value is a social arrangement that has opposite consequences for the happiness and well-being of children and the gratification and self-actualization of adults. A possible, though by no means certain, example of this is unilateral no-fault divorce. In such a case, assessment of the derivative value cannot be made on a strictly empirical basis; a judgment must be made about the relative importance of the two ultimate values. Therefore, some of the conflict in the family wars grows out of neither disagreement about empirical matters nor adherence to different ultimate values. Rather, it results from differences in the importance assigned to different ultimate values.

The fact that the same derivative value sometimes relates to more than one ultimate value is almost certainly an important source of bias in the interpretation of social scientific evidence. Rather than recognizing that an arrangement or policy has contradictory consequences for two ultimate values and experiencing the dissonance involved in having to decide between the two values, a person may discount the evidence for the effects on one of the values. For instance, in the example given above, a person may not want to admit to self or others that he or she considers anything more important than either the happiness and well-being of children or the gratification and self actualization of adults. Indeed, in the debates about unilateral no-fault divorce, there seems to be a strong tendency for participants on both sides to believe that the effects are similar for adults and children; mention of possible adult-child conflicts of interest has been rare.

The intrusion of the kinds of bias discussed here is facilitated by the ambiguity of much social scientific evidence. Social scientists can rarely conduct randomized experiments—the kind of research that can provide the strongest evidence for causation. For instance, in assessing the effects of parental divorce on children, researchers cannot randomly divide a population of children into an experimental group, whose parents are made to divorce, and a control group, from which the experimental stimulus of parental divorce is withheld. Instead, they must settle for a quasi-experimental design, in which they attempt statistically to hold constant effects on child outcomes other than those from parental divorce-nondivorce. Because it is not possible to know that all other effects have been equalized, quasi-experimental research cannot yield conclusive evidence of causation. And when there is moderate to strong but not definitive evidence for a causal relationship, which is the best that quasi-experimental research can provide, the ideological predispositions of the researchers and others who interpret the evidence can lead either to a dogmatic conclusion that the relationship exists or to an unwarranted dismissal of the evidence. For instance, the correct statement that "there is no conclusive evidence" for a particular effect can be embedded in a dismissive context to create the impression that it does not, or probably does not, exist.

Consideration of these barriers to an accurate assessment of the empirical claims on which derivative values are based might lead one to embrace the often-repeated postmodernist cliche that "there is no such thing as objectivity." In a sense, that claim is true; perfect objectivity is an unattainable ideal. Bias cannot be completely eliminated; we can only hope for varying degrees of approximation of objectivity.

Contrary to some postmodernist thought, however, the degree of that approximation matters. The quest for objectivity is noble and worthwhile—just as worthwhile as the equally difficult quest for justice. It is worthwhile because only by perceiving the nature of social and psychological reality with reasonable accuracy can activists, reformers, policy makers, and others devise effective means to change that reality in accordance with the ultimate values to which they are committed. Those who would make the world a better place sabotage the attainment of their own goals if they let bias distort their perceptions of reality.

Fortunately, the norm of objectivity remains strong among a core of the best social scientists, among whom those who study controversial family issues have often let their examination of the evidence lead them to conclusions unpopular in academic circles. I turn now to some salient examples of scientific integrity among family researchers.

Evidence of Scientific Integrity among Family Scholars

Given the pervasive liberal ethos among social scientists and scholars in the humanities and the applied fields related to the social sciences, the most obvious cases of integrity are those in which researchers have let the evidence lead them to conclusions unpopular in liberal circles—especially when the persons have reversed their earlier conclusions. Of course, scientific integrity may often, or even usually, lead to "liberal" conclusions, but such instances are more difficult to detect. In the family field, obvious cases of such integrity would have to be found among the few scholars with known strong conservative biases and social ties. The cases discussed here all involve rejection of orthodox liberal views, but I do not mean to imply that scientific integrity must always lead to that outcome.

Eminent social demographer Andrew Cherlin of Johns Hopkins University wrote extensively about family policy issues but remained somewhat aloof from the ideological debates until 1991. In that year, he and six other scholars published an article in the prestigious journal *Science* in which they presented findings from analyses of U. S. and British data indicating that most of the apparent negative effects of divorce on children resulted from pre-separation parental conflict rather than from the separation, divorce, and the aftermath of separation and divorce.² This conclusion was of course seized upon by liberal commentators to support their sanguine views of divorce, and anti-divorce conservatives, while not challenging the empirical data, strongly criticized the pro-divorce implications drawn from them. One such criticism, by Richard Gill in an article in the *Public Interest*,³ drew a sharp response from Cherlin, who then became identified as a liberal partisan in the family wars.

It was thus notable when, in 1995 and again in 1998, articles by Cherlin and two co-authors, published in *Demography*⁴ and the *American Sociological Review*,⁵ reported conclusions rather different from those in the *Science* article. An extended analysis of the British data set used for the earlier study still indicated that pre-parental-separation family characteristics had some negative effects on the mental health of the children of divorce, but the new research estimated greater effects from the divorce and its aftermath. The first article reported this finding for persons up to age twenty-three and the second for those up to age thirty-three. Cherlin must have known that these findings would be used by his former critics to support their ideological agenda, but this did not deter him from reporting them.

A somewhat similar case is that of sociologists Paul Amato and Alan Booth, both of Pennsylvania State University. Like Cherlin, these two scholars are cautious researchers known for balanced and objective interpretations of the evidence. Much of Amato's and Booth's work has been widely cited by both "concerned" and "sanguine" interpreters of recent family trends to support their positions. For instance, concerned scholars have often cited a 1991 meta-analysis by Amato and Bruce Keith⁶ that indicates consistent evidence for negative effects of divorce and its aftermath on a large number of child outcomes, while sanguine scholars have often cited the same piece as evidence that any effects are rather small. By the late 1990s, Amato in particular was receiving considerable favorable attention from liberal authors—attention that must have been to some degree gratifying—when he and Booth published *A Generation at Risk*,⁷ the 1997 Harvard University Press book that arguably dealt the greatest blow of the decade to the sanguine position concerning divorce.

The research reported in that book indicated that in most cases of divorce involving children, there was not enough pre-separation conflict to be greatly harmful to children and that the latter would have benefited from their parents' staying together, at least until the offspring reached adulthood. This conclusion contradicts the belief, very widely held by both family social scientists and lay persons, that adults in unhappy marriages cannot benefit their children by staying together and thus should not delay or forgo divorce for the sake of the children. This belief is very comforting to divorced parents, and thus reporting evidence contrary to it was bound to be very unpopular in some circles, including among the liberal scholars who had given Amato much favorable attention. It was very courageous, therefore, for Amato and Booth to conclude that "Spending one-third of one's life living in a marriage that is less than satisfactory in order to benefit children—children that parents elected to bring into the world—is not an unreasonable expectation...."[8] (p. 238).

Such instances of obvious scientific integrity have not been especially rare. The case of Sara McLanahan, a one-time radical and single parent who became convinced by the evidence that the increased prevalence of single parenthood was having negative effects on children, was chronicled in the influential 1993 *Atlantic Monthly* article by Barabara Dafoe Whitehead titled "Dan Quayle Was Right."[9] I need only add that McLanahan has resisted letting the favorable attention she received from conservatives seduce her into embracing the derivative values of extreme conservatism. Another instance is the 1997 Harvard University Press book by Susan Mayer of the University of Chicago titled *What Money Can't Buy.*[10] In that book Mayer reports several ingenious analyses that control for unmeasured variables in order to separate the effects of money from those of other influences on child outcomes. A major conclusion is that to a large extent the negative outcomes for poor children result not from poverty but from parental characteristics that commonly cause the poverty and the negative child outcomes. That this politically incorrect finding did not result from a conservative bias is evidenced by Mayer's policy recommendations, which follow liberal, welfare state lines.

I could continue with examples, but these few are sufficient to illustrate that there is a hard core of competent social scientists committed to the ideal of objectivity and to letting the evidence lead where it may, regardless of where they would like it to lead. The instances of integrity cited are not in themselves "uses" of social science findings, of course, but they provide the basis for appropriate uses for personal and policy decisions and tend to improve the quality of public discourse on family issues.

My purpose here is to demonstrate that the promotion of constructive uses of social science findings is not futile and that a fairly close approximation of objectivity is not an unattainable goal, at least among persons who are properly socialized in the norms of science.

Misuses of the Findings of Family Social Science

Although they are not reason for despair, misuses and misinterpretations of family social science findings are also common. Even the findings reported by the most responsible researchers, such as those whose work is described above, have been used irresponsibly by activists in the family debates. The latter have tended to push the conclusions to extremes not supported by the evidence and to overlook the fact that even the conclusions drawn from the best of research may be incorrect. The quasi-experimental studies that must be used to investigate family phenomena can only *suggest*, or at most *indicate*, cause and effect and can never conclusively *prove* it. Stated differently, the researchers can only *infer* causation from their findings and from the unproven assumptions they must make, either explicitly or implicitly, when they do research; they do not *find* effects. When researchers fail to state their causal conclusions with appropriate tentativeness, as even the best ones are prone to do, they invite misuses of their findings by activists. The strongest conclusion usually warranted by the evidence on an issue is that "the preponderance of the evidence indicates _____." Such a conclusion must be sufficient to spur activism and policy recommendations, of course, because stronger well-based conclusions will usually not be forthcoming.

More serious than overly strong conclusions are those contrary to the evidence or based on flawed research, several of which have been used extensively in the family wars. Here I discuss a few cases to illustrate different ways in which such inappropriate uses of social science can come about. In specific cases, however, one cannot be certain of the motivations of those responsible for the misuses, and therefore I can only suggest that each illustration fits the cause with which I associate it.

Some misuses of social science findings result from nothing more than poorly conducted research and the inability of activists to assess the quality of the research. An apparent case of activists unknowingly using conclusions based on flawed research occurred after the 1995 publication in the *Journal of Marriage and the Family* of the results of a study designed to estimate the effects of no-fault divorce on divorce rates in the fifty United States.[11] Although the study had the patina of sophistication, with the inclusion of several control variables in some of the analyses, the estimate of the effect for each state was merely the difference between the mean divorce rate for the three years prior to enactment of no-fault divorce and the mean for the three years following enactment. This difference is a patently inadequate estimate of the effect, being based implicitly on the absurd assumption that nothing else happened to influence the divorce rate during the seven-year period covered by the data. Yet these estimates of effects have been very extensively used in the "divorce reform movement" aimed at limiting access to no-fault divorce, being cited, for instance, in hearings on proposed legislation in several states. More appropriate research on the effects of no-fault divorce indicates that enactment probably did moderately increase the divorce rate in some states.[12] However, it is fallacious to argue, as some activists have done, that if enactment of no-fault provisions led to an increase in divorce, rescinding those provisions would necessarily lead to a corresponding reduction. Some effects are irreversible, or largely so.

A somewhat different situation is when activists are willing to further their causes by using the results of research they know to be flawed. When this happens, the persons are more committed to derivative values than to ultimate ones, or else they have faith not based on empirical evidence in the efficacy of the policies they advocate. I do not give an example, because it is impossible to know when this happens.

On other occasions unsupported conclusions are disseminated and used in the ideological debates because social scientific researchers, impelled by their natural desire to draw attention to their work and to themselves, leap to dramatic and attention-getting conclusions that are at best only weakly suggested by their findings and at worst are nothing more than conjecture. The refereeing process tends to minimize such conclusions in papers published in professional journals, so they come largely from interviews with media representatives or from nonrefereed publications.

A case that probably falls within this category is that of a young sociologist who did a study of trends in the "intergenerational transmission of divorce," the conclusions from which were reported in a press release from his university in 1999. Using data from the General Social Surveys, the sociologist looked at the difference in percentage of ever-married persons who had ever been divorced or separated between the "children of divorce" and persons who lived with both biological or adoptive parents at age sixteen. The percentage was higher for the children of divorce from the early 1970s through the middle 1990s, but the difference was smaller at the end of that period than at the beginning. This trend persisted after introduction of controls for time exposed to the risk of divorce and several variables known to be associated with the probability of divorcing. A generally responsible report of this well-conducted research appeared in the journal *Demography*,[13] the article being marred only by rather implausible speculation about the reasons for the trend and a neglect of earlier literature that had predicted it and had given reasons why the change would occur.

However, the university press release, which the sociologist presumably saw and approved, heralded a decrease in the divorce rate of the children of divorce. In fact, the study showed no such change, nor did it deal with divorce rates at all, the percentage of ever-married persons who had ever been divorced or separated being a reflection of divorce rates at various times over the past several decades. Furthermore, this percentage *increased* for the children of divorce during the period covered by the study; the convergence reported occurred only because the percentage increased even more for persons whose parents did not divorce. Nevertheless, the incorrect statement that the divorce rate had decreased for the children of divorce appeared in many newspapers and magazines, including the *New York Times*,[14] and has been used by activists to argue that divorce is no longer as serious a problem as it once was. Much of the press coverage included the sociologist's speculation that the indicated trend resulted from a decline in the stigma associated with divorce, even though to my knowledge no other scholar has suggested that stigma is a mechanism through which the intergenerational transmission of divorce occurs.

Considering this study against the backdrop of earlier research and theorizing on the intergenerational transmission of divorce makes clear that a facile jump from its findings to sanguine conclusions about divorce is not warranted. One of the possible and probable reasons for the transmission most frequently mentioned in the literature is that the children of divorce, having experienced and observed the problems in their parents' marriage, tend to be fearful of marriage and to lack confidence in its stability and thus find it hard to make the commitments and "investments" needed for marital success. As divorce became more common, this negative influence is likely to have spread to persons who saw divorce all around them as they grew up even though their own parents did not divorce. Consistent with this speculation is the fact that the difference in divorce proneness between the children of divorce and others has been less in high-divorce segments of the population, such as among blacks and in high-divorce regions of the country, than among other people.[15] If this view is correct, the convergence in divorce proneness found by the 1999 study is hardly good news.

Probably the most important reasons why incorrect and insufficiently supported conclusions are reported and used in ideological debates are those I discuss above, including especially the desire of researchers to gain the approval of their ideological compatriots. Given the pervasive liberal preferences of social scientists, some tendency for interpretations of evidence to be slanted toward views popular among liberals is virtually certain. It is almost certain that poorly conducted research is more likely to be reported in the professional journals if it leads to sanguine conclusions about family change, even though the no-fault divorce study discussed above does not fit that pattern.

A probable instance of a study that would not have gotten exposure in a respected journal if it had led to a less popular conclusion is one reported in the *Journal of Family Psychology* in 1999.[16] The researcher addressed the question of whether or not fatherlessness has adverse effects on children by looking at achievement outcomes among six-year-olds and seven-year-olds and concluded that he could find no evidence for negative effects. However, "fatherlessness" was defined merely as living in a household without an adult male, so that children with stepfathers or whose mothers had live-in boyfriends were not considered fatherless, in spite of ample evidence that such men typically do not relate to children in the same way as biological or adoptive fathers. Furthermore, fatherlessness, as defined, was measured only at age six or seven, whereas the family history of the child was much more important than his or her current living situation. For instance, a child whose mother had just recently divorced was coded as fatherless while one who had never lived with an adult male until recently was coded as not fatherless. Finally, a great deal of the evidence on the effects of family structure on child achievement indicates that the main effects become apparent only at ages older than six or seven. In spite of these flaws in the study, its main conclusion received much play in the press, and the *New York Times* opined that the study gave single parents one less thing to worry about.[17]

These misuses of family social science findings are among the most conspicuous ones in recent years, but dozens of similar misuses have occurred in the United States during the course of the family wars.

Maximizing Appropriate Uses and Minimizing Misuses of Social Science Findings

The ultimate purpose of discussing constructive and inappropriate uses of social science findings is of course to try to contribute to an increase of the ratio of the former to the latter. My consideration of the matter leads me to suggest several steps that social scientists and other concerned persons could and should take to achieve that goal.

Social scientists should, for instance, work through their professional associations for greater attention in codes of ethics to the responsibility of researchers to do everything they can to see that the findings of their research are reported accurately and interpreted correctly in the media and in educational materials, such as textbooks. The codes should stress such matters as the obligation of researchers to assure that press releases issued by their universities accurately report their work. Perhaps imposing an ethical obligation on researchers to monitor textbooks would be going too far, but researchers could and should do that, and they should complain to authors and publishers about the flaws they find.

Social scientists and other concerned persons should also monitor media reports of social science findings and respond by writing op-ed pieces and letters to editors when they detect misinterpretations and distortions of evidence. Of course, there are honest differences of opinion about issues of interpretation among social scientists devoted to the ideal of objectivity, and there are similar disagreements about what evidence is worth reporting. When there is not a consensus among competent and respected scholars, that fact, and the debates among the scholars, should be made public.

University administrators and others who evaluate and reward social scientists should recognize the importance of accurate and responsible communication of social science findings to the public and to policymakers. Those who perform this service well, for instance by writing quality textbooks and articles for popular magazines such as *American Demographics* and *Psychology Today*, should be highly rewarded for doing so. Perhaps this function should be almost as highly rewarded as doing important research, because without it, research has limited value.

Professional associations in the social sciences should give more attention to the dissemination of social scientific findings to those who can use them for personal and policy decisions. This dissemination now occurs through means over which the academic disciplines and their professional associations exercise little influence. These associations should sponsor journals devoted to the publication of refereed popularizations of social science research and theory.

Such journals would not of course be free from ideological bias, but I have confidence that the hard core of professionals in each discipline devoted to the ideals of science would keep them from coming under the control of any particular ideological or political faction.

Social scientists should join with departments of journalism to give fledgling journalists better training in the scientific method and in the special methodological problems that plague social and psychological research. Too many journalists and other media representatives do not understand even such basics as the difference between correlation and causation or the fact that nonexperimental research cannot prove causation.

Social scientists cannot remain aloof from ideological debates, and they should not try to do so, but they should, insofar as possible, make sure that their most important "significant others" are those who value objectivity and consider changing one's mind on a controversial issue to be a badge of honor rather than an occasion for embarrassment. Affiliation with think tanks and organizations that have an ideological agenda may help social scientists promote constructive uses of social science evidence, but only if they are not reluctant to oppose bias within those organizations. Social scientists with such ties should constantly guard against letting devotion to derivative values sabotage commitment to their ultimate values.

Professional socialization in graduate programs in the social sciences should give greater attention than it typically does to the issues discussed here. Particularly important in such socialization is the discussion of such issues as the distinction between ultimate and derivative values and the need to avoid dogmatic adherence to the latter. Training in dealing with the media should be a central part of the socialization of fledgling social scientists.

These steps, suggested by examination of the family wars and family-related social research, should help to maximize constructive uses and minimize misuses of all kinds of social science findings.

Notes

1. The distinction between ultimate and derivative values is one that I have used for many years and probably did not originate with me. However, I have been unable to identify its source.
2. Andrew J. Cherlin, Frank F. Furstenberg, Jr., P. Lindsay Chase-Lansdale, Kathleen E. Kiernan, Philip K. Robins, Donna Ruane Morrison, and Julien O. Teitler, "Longitudinal Studies of Effects of Divorce on Children in Great Britain and the United States, *Science*, Vol. 252 (June 7, 1991): 1386-1389.
3. Richard T. Gill, "For the Sake of the Children," *Public Interest*, Volume 111 (Spring, 1993): 86-94.
4. Andrew J. Cherlin, Kathleen E. Kiernan, and P. Lindsay Chase-Lansdale, "Parental Divorce in Childhood and Demographic Outcomes in Young Adulthood," *Demography*, Vol. 32 (August, 1995): 299-318.
5. Andrew J. Cherlin, P. Lindsay Chase-Landsdale, and Christine McRae, "Effects of Parental Divorce on Mental Health Throughout the Life Course," *American Sociological Review*, Vol. 63 (April, 1998): 239-249.
6. Paul Amato and Bruce Keith, "Parental Divorce and the Well-being of Chidlren," *Psychological Bulletin*, Vol. 110 (July, 1991): 26-46.
7. Paul Amato and Alan Booth, *A Generation at Risk: Growing Up in an Era of Family Upheaval*, Cambridge, MA: Harvard University Press, 1997.
8. Ibid., p. 238.
9. Barbara Dafoe Whitehead, "Dan Quayle Was Right," *Atlantic Monthly*, April, 1993, pp. 47-84.
10. Susan E. Mayer, *What Money Can't Buy: Family Income and Children's Life Chances*, Cambridge, MA: Harvard University Press, 1997.
11. Paul. A. Nakonezny, Robert D. Shull, and Joseph L. Rodgers, "The Effect of No-fault Divorce Law on the Divorce Rate across the 50 States and Its Relation to Income, Education, and Religiosity," *Journal of Marriage and the Family*, Vol. 57 (May, 1995): 477-488.
12. Leora Friedberg, "Did Unilateral Divorce Raise Divorce Rates? Evidence from Panel Data," *American Economic Review*, Vol. 88 (June, 1998): 608-627.
13. Nicholas Wolfinger, "Trends in the Intergenerational Transmission of Divorce," *Demography*, Vol. 36 (August, 1999): 415-420.
14. "Good News for the Children of Divorce," *New York Times*, August 17, 1999.
15. Norval Glenn and Kathryn Kramer, "The Marriages and Divorces of the Children of Divorce," *Journal of Marriage and the Family*, Vol. 49 (November, 1987): 811-825.

16. Henry Ricciuti, "Single Parrenhood and School Readiness in White, Black, and Hispanic 6- and 7-Year Olds." *Journal of Family Psychology,* Vol. 13 (September, 1999): 450-465.
17. "For Single Parents, One Less Worry," *New York Times*, October 5, 1999.

7

Environmental Cancer

Stanley Rothman and S. Robert Lichter

Cancer has been called the "dread disease." Americans fear it like no other illness. It sneaks up silently, is cruel and painful, and all too often results in bodily mutilation and/or death. Considerable progress has been made recently in both the diagnosis and treatment of many cancers, and scientists are cautiously optimistic about discovering more effective treatments. Furthermore, age-adjusted cancer rates have begun to decline for the first time since the 1930s, at least in part because of the drop-off in smoking by men. However, all too often today once the disease is diagnosed there is little that can be done except to make the patient as comfortable as possible.

Even as our knowledge of the nature and causes of cancer accumulates, key issues surrounding the disease(s) are still being debated and have become embroiled in politics. Given that most cancers are triggered by environmental factors (broadly defined), issues of public policy can not help being involved. For example, as our ability to detect ever-smaller amounts of carcinogenic materials in our environment increases, a number of questions present themselves with increasing force. What proportion of cancers have their source in man-made carcinogens? Has modern industrial society produced an increase in cancer rates? What dosage of suspected carcinogens is dangerous? What methods shall we use to measure cancer potential? Are tests using mice or rats applicable to human beings? How and to what extent should we control potentially cancer causing activities?

Views about cancer and other environmental issues influence public policy and determine how much money is spent on what. Obviously, public and private funds are not unlimited and we have to make choices. Money spent on cleaning up toxic dumps is not available for AIDS or breast cancer research, building new schools, or Medicaid.

In the United States the key public elite groups involved in making decisions about both funding and regulation are members of Congress, the president, judges, and bureaucrats. However, other elite groups from the private sector are also heavily involved in influencing what courses of action are chosen. These include industry lobbyists, environmental activists, the mass media, and the scientific community. What roles do these groups play in influencing public opinion and hence public policy? Who decides which scientific studies get the most public attention?

We address here aspects of the controversy surrounding the question of environmental cancer, emphasizing the interactions among environmental activists, scientists, and the news media. We want to know how the scientific community conceives of environmental cancer and its risks and to what extent their findings accord with the views of mainstream environmental organizations. We also want to know how accurately the media report the views of scientific experts on environmental cancer, and, in general, to what extent the consensus of the expert community is reflected in the risk assumptions underlying public policy.

In 1993 we surveyed a random sample of 400 members of the American Association of Cancer Researchers (AACR) who specialize either in carcinogenesis or epidemiology. Our response rate was 65 percent. The study replicated (with slight variations) a random survey of cancer epidemiologists and oncologists completed in 1984.

Our sample was primarily made up of academics. Sixty-three percent of our respondents were on the faculties of a medical school or had another university affiliation. Another 13 percent worked for a government agency. Only 7 percent worked in private industry. Of those not working in private industry 73 percent had *never* served as consultants for industry; only 8 percent had done so more than three times. Those we interviewed were actively involved in research and publication. Ninety-two percent were currently involved in research on cancer causation or prevention. Fifty-five percent have published forty or more articles in professional journals.

Politically, the scientists tend to the liberal side of the spectrum. Forty-eight percent classify themselves as liberal; 28 percent classify themselves as moderate and a mere 17 percent consider themselves conservatives. At the same time a substantial majority consider themselves Democrats or lean toward the Democratic Party. The results are hardly surprising given that the scientists are predominantly academics even if some may also be MDs.

Expert Views on Environmental Cancer

The cancer experts were asked (among a great many other things) to evaluate the contribution of various aspects of the environment, including man-made substances, to human cancer rates in the United States. They rated each aspect on a scale of zero to ten, where "zero" indicates that something makes no contribution to cancer rates, and "ten" indicates that it makes a very important contribution.

In presenting the experts' ratings on this dimension, we rank environmental agents according to the average (mean) score that they received. We also discuss the proportion of scientists who rated each choice as a "major" cause (7 to 10 on the scale), a "moderate" (4 to 6) cause, or a "minor" cause (0 to 3). Cancer experts place tobacco in a league of its own among cancer agents. Indeed, only one out of twenty researchers rate smoking as less than a major carcinogen. Chewing tobacco is named as a major carcinogen by 66 percent of the scientists. That rating placed this form of tobacco well ahead of asbestos, the only other substance named as a major cancer agent by a majority (56 percent) of experts. (Sunlight, though, of course, not a man-made agent, is rated as a major cause of cancer by 54 percent of our respondents and receives an average score of 6.33 out of 10).

Second-hand tobacco smoke is the only other substance deemed a major cause of cancer by a plurality of cancer experts (46 percent). Thus, various forms of tobacco accounted for three of the top four substances on this rating list. No other substance was rated as a major contributor to cancer rates by more than about one-third of those in the sample. Nor did any of the thirteen other substances receive a mean rating above 5.4 on the scale.

A cluster of six additional substances elicited a lower level of concern, with mean ratings ranging from roughly 4.6 to 5.4. In descending order, these included fat in the diet, the natural chemical aflatoxin, low fiber in the diet, dioxin, air and water pollution, and alcohol. About one in three scientists rated high fat diets, aflatoxin, and dioxin as major contributors to cancer rates, compared to one in four who expressed as much concern about low dietary fiber and air and water pollution. But dioxin's average rating dropped below that of both dietary factors, owing to the relatively large proportion of experts (40 percent) who rated it as only a minor cause of cancer. Beginning with dioxin, the remaining ten substances were all rated as minor causes of cancer by a plurality of those experts who expressed an opinion, except for air and water pollution where a plurality felt they were a medium cause of cancer. Five of these were clustered with in one increment on the rating scale—alcohol, EDB (ethylene dibromide a pesticide), radon (a naturally occurring radioactive gas), hormone treatments, and DDT (another pesticide).

The scientists expressed the least concern about four substances whose cancer-causing potential has generated headlines, but which they consensually regarded as only minor contributors to cancer rates. Nuclear power, the pesticide Alar, saccharine, and other artificial sweeteners generated mean ratings ranging from only about 1.2 to 2.5. All were regarded as minor cancer agents by large majorities, the size of which ranged from 64 percent (Alar) to 83 percent (sweeteners other than saccharin). No more than 7 percent of cancer experts rated any of these substances as a major contributor to cancer rates. Tobacco and asbestos were rated by far the most dangerous substances in terms of their contribution to cancer rates, scoring higher even than sunlight.

These are almost exactly the same results as those obtained in the 1984 study conducted by Stanley Rothman and William Lunch. Thus they seem to reflect a long-term consensus rather than a recent shift of scientific opinion. There is little difference in opinion between those scientists who have consulted with industry and those who have not and women seem to be slightly more risk adverse than are men. However, the largest differences vary with scholarly publication. The more articles published by a researcher the *less* likely he or she is to rank such substances as dioxin or DDT or EDB or food additives as major carcinogens. Thus those researchers who have published twenty or fewer articles rate dioxin as 5.5 on our 10 point scale, whereas scientists who have published fifty or more articles rate it as 4.1. The same is true for DDT where the ratings are 4.4 and 3.3 respectively.

We should stress that researchers are by no means unanimous in their judgments. There are even a few experts who still believe that tobacco is not a major source of lung cancer. One suspects some disagreement will always be found on scientific issues associated with public policy. Nevertheless on many issues the level of agreement is impressive.

Environmentalist Views on Cancer Causes

We may compare these results with the positions taken by a sample of leading environmentalists from the major environmental organizations of whom we asked many of the same questions. Environmental leaders assigned higher risks than cancer researchers to eleven out of thirteen substances listed on which their estimates were compared. Only tobacco (smoking) and sunlight attracted slightly more concern from the researchers. In the case of man-made substances, the differences in their ratings were frequently dramatic. At least twice as many activists as scientists detected "major" cancer threats from Alar, artificial sweeteners, DDT, dioxin, food additives, and nuclear power plants.

The differences were even greater at the other end of the scale, with scientists far more likely than activists to rate most substances as relatively "minor" causes of cancer. Thus, using the mean score of carcinogenicity, about twice as many researchers as environmentalists rated Alar and nuclear power as minor carcinogens; three times as many researchers placed DDT and asbestos at the low end of the scale; five times as many researchers regarded food additives and dioxin as minor threats; and a whopping seventeen times as many cancer specialists as environmental leaders (by 34 to 2 percent) saw pollution as a minor contributor to cancer rates. Interestingly, the ratings of scientists and activists do not differ that much on natural sources of cancer. It is on man-made potential carcinogens that the differences are really substantial.

How has this disparity between expert and activist opinion affected public perception on the issue? Specifically, how have the media communicated these debates to the general public and how accurately do the media messages represent the views of the scientific community on these issues? To ascertain this, we selected a representative sample of the most visible reports from television, news magazines, and leading newspapers. Specifically, we examined all news stories on this topic that appeared on the ABC, CBS, and NBC evening newscasts or in *Time*, *Newsweek*, and *U.S. News and World Report*, as well as stories on the front page of any section of the *New York Times*, *Washington Post*, and *Wall Street Journal*, between 1972 and 1992. This produced a total sample of 1,206 news items.

The patterns of media coverage are very complicated and change over time. However, in general, the most serious sources of cancer in terms of frequency of mention in the mass media (including attribution to scientists) are quite at variance with the demonstrated views of the scientific community.

Man-made chemicals head the list of carcinogens mentioned by media sources, whether or not the sources are identified as "expert." While tobacco is mentioned quite frequently, sunlight and dietary choices are quite low on the list of those factors covered. Just as important, media coverage of various controversies about cancer is very much at odds with those of the scientific community and much closer to that of the environmentalist community. For example, a very large majority of sources cited by the media argue that we face a cancer epidemic. Yet less than a third of the cancer researchers surveyed believe that to be the case.

The pattern is repeated on other controversial issues. For example, consider the question as to whether cancer-causing agents are unsafe at any dose. As a technical question, this involves the determination of tolerance levels for carcinogenic substances. A catchword of toxicology is the adage that the dose determines the poison, and most researchers apply this principle to suspected cancer agents. Only 28 percent of scientists surveyed concurred with the assertion that carcinogens are unsafe regardless of dose (64 percent disagreed, with the rest undecided). If one turns to media coverage of the issues, however, one comes away with the opposite impression. Some 66 percent of media sources agree that cancer causing agents are unsafe at any dose.

Can the results of animal studies of suspected carcinogens be extrapolated to humans in order to assess the health risks associated with specific substances? This is a standard procedure for establishing carcinogenicity in accordance with federal regulations. The approach has long been controversial, because it involves giving very high doses of substances to animals and extrapolating the results to humans who are exposed to far lower doses of the same substance. When we put this question to the expert community, the result was close to a consensual rejection of these procedures and the assumptions they involve. Only one in four cancer researchers (27 percent) endorsed the practice of assessing human cancer risks by giving animals what is termed the "maximum tolerable dose" of suspected cancer-causing agents. More than double that number (63 percent) disagreed, with the remainder unsure. According to the major media's quoted sources, however, the situation is more ambiguous, with 50 percent agreeing that these animal tests are adequate to assess the dangers of suspected carcinogens. One can, of course, argue that in the absence of good epidemiological data, we must use animal studies. That is no excuse, however, for giving the impression that such results are more solid than they actually are.

Finally, we asked scientists to evaluate the "zero risk" standard embodied in the now partly superseded Delaney Clause, which required that chemicals and additives must be banned from food and drugs if they were shown to produce tumors in any species. This principle sparked public controversy ever since it led to the FDA's decision to ban saccharin in 1977, a decision which was never implemented because of public protest. But the research community rejected this principle by an overwhelming seven to one margin (85 percent disagreed with the Delaney Clause and only 12 percent supported it, with the rest unsure). The impression given by the media is similar, but some 25 percent of the experts cited by them supported the Delaney clause, twice as many as did in our sample.

In summary, large majorities of the research community reject as overly risk-aversive several propositions and practices that currently guide environmental cancer policy. Most cancer experts dismiss the popular notion of a cancer epidemic in America, and they attribute the most significant factor in the (until recently) observable rise in cancer rates to tobacco use, sunlight, diet and aging rather than the products of modern industry.

Most researchers at the time of our study also rejected some of the principles that underlie the current regulatory approach to environmental cancer. These included the inference of human cancer risk from animal tests involving high dosages of suspected carcinogens, the idea that cancer-causing agents are unsafe at any dose, and the analogous "zero risk" regulatory standard for evaluating food and drugs. It should be noted, however, that not all cancer experts reject such views. Many competent scientists accept at least some of them. It is, of course, rare for any scientific controversy involving public policy to produce unanimity. Media reports gave a quite different impression. In fact, on those issues for which we have data, they are much closer to the views of environmental activists than they are to the views of the scientists we surveyed. For example, 39 percent of activists supported the Delaney clause; over 60 percent believed we are facing a cancer epidemic, and over 50 percent believe that cancer-causing agents are unsafe at any level.

It is little wonder that scientists regard media reporting of cancer issues as very poor. It may come as no surprise that only one out of sixteen scientists in our sample (6 percent) rate television news as a highly reliable source of information on environmental cancer, while nearly ten times as many (55 percent) rate television newscasts as unreliable sources. But the ratings were hardly any better for the weekly newsmagazines, despite their advantages of running longer stories on more leisurely deadlines. Only 9 percent of cancer experts rate newsmagazines highly, compared to 49 percent who give them low reliability ratings.

Most striking of all, though, is the lack of scientific respect for the *New York Times*, which is renowned among journalists for its award-winning weekly science section. Fewer than one in four researchers (22 percent) rate the *Times* as highly reliable in its cancer coverage. In fact, the proportion of cancer experts who rate America's paper of record as unreliable exceeded the proportion who found it highly reliable by 30 percent to 22 percent. As a baseline for comparison, 54 percent rated *Scientific American* as highly reliable, while only 8 percent call it unreliable.

Nor does the scientific community have much respect for most of the scientists cited most frequently by the media as sources of information about cancer. Only 24 percent of the scientists polled express relatively high confidence in Sidney Wolfe and Samuel Epstein, two of the most widely quoted media sources, and frequently cited as experts by environmentalist organizations. On the other hand, 67 percent of the scientists polled express great confidence in Berkeley biochemist Bruce Ames, who is regarded as a lackey of business by many activists. Close behind Dr. Ames in reputational ratings are Richard Peto and Richard Doll, whose conclusions about cancer causation are quite similar to those of Ames. (In fact, based on mean ratings that excluded respondents who did not rate each individual, Doll finished slightly ahead of Ames atop the list, while Epstein fell slightly behind Dr. Wolfe at the very bottom.)

Some of the major environmental groups receive similarly poor ratings. Only 16 percent of the scientists rate the Environmental Defense Fund highly, as compared to 92 percent who give high ratings to the National Cancer Institute or the 87 percent who give that rating to the National Institutes of Health. Interestingly, a large proportion of scientists do not feel that they know enough about the two activist groups listed (Center for Science in the Public Interest and Environmental Defense Fund) to even rate them.

Why are the views of environmental activists so different from those of the scientific community on the dangers of man-made sources of cancer, though not on natural causes? Clearly many factors are involved, though scientific illiteracy does not seem to be a key variable. We argue that the views of some environmental activists derive in part from a broader set of political and social attitudes. The leaders of the mainstream environmental groups are not as far to the left as are the leaders of some of the more radical environmental groups, or as were an earlier generation of mainstream environmental leaders. They are, however, well to the left of the general population, as well as of scientists, so far as we can determine.

Our survey reveals that environmental activists characterize themselves as very liberal across the board, and they are very suspicious of business. They also favor extensive governmental economic intervention. Thus, their belief that contemporary capitalism produces cancer may well be partially the manifestation of a broader critical view of their society. Of course, the cancer researchers in our sample, which is largely composed of academics or government scientists, also hold liberal views on social issues, though we can not easily compare them directly with environmentalists. However, their political orientation does not, by and large, carry over to their area of expertise.

Further, they seem relatively moderate as compared to the environmental activists whose views contrast sharply with that of the general population on a wide range of subjects including environmental issues. This is true despite the public's general environmental concern and the respect with which they regard environmental activists. For example, while 61 percent of the general public believe that government regulation of business is harmful, only 6 percent of the environmentalists share that view. Similarly, 40 percent of the public believes that business attempts to balance profits and the public interest, double the proportion (19 percent) of environmental leaders who agree.

And why have reporters turned to the environmental groups for news about the environment and believed them rather than others? There are clearly many reasons for such behavior, not the least of which is the ability of environmental groups to organize effectively, and (though this can be exaggerated) journalists' penchant for "bad" news as well as the reality of environmental degradation. A penchant for bad news, however, does not explain the 1950s willingness of the media to side with the scientific establishment on the fluoridation controversy of that period or to have reported the AIDS controversy with such care and sympathy, stressing that casual contact with an AIDS victim is not dangerous and convincing the general public of that fact.

As Mary Douglas and Aaron Wildavsky pointed out in 1982 in *Risk and Culture: An Essay on the Selection of Technical and Environmental Dangers*, it is equally hard to make the case that concern about, say, pesticides is merely a function of a particular type of risk assessment engaged in by laymen as against scientists. People are more willing to take risks they conceive of as being imposed by themselves (e.g., driving an automobile) than those they perceive as imposed on them by others (e.g., the use of pesticides). However this pattern should not affect *estimates* of risk, especially estimates by environmental activists who have been working in the field for some time.

At least some critics have argued that media reportage can be explained, paradoxically, by the very professionalism of journalists who are trained to believe that there are two sides to every issue. But it is difficult to argue that professional norms lead to giving equal credence to positions that are rejected by most experts in the field, or by reporting on issues in such a way as to lead the public to believe that a majority of experts supports a given risk assessment when the experts actually do not. Indeed, our content analysis reveals that, in stories about environmental cancer, assertions that a given substance is a dangerous carcinogen are given far more play than are those which are more skeptical. Furthermore, we compared those stories in which reporters do not attribute views to any one in particular, but simply state them as conclusions, to those in which such statements are specifically attributed to one or another expert. The results were the same. According to media stories the views of experts closely resemble those of environmental activists on almost every important issue.

There are, of course, other elements in the equation. Studies show that many scientists are suspicious of journalists because they conceive of them is irresponsible and inaccurate in their reporting. If journalists cannot obtain the information that they desire from mainstream scientists they are more likely than otherwise to turn to environmental groups which are eager to attract their attention. Mainstream scientists are unlikely to be willing to speculate outside their fields. They are very concerned that the technical discussion of their findings should be accurate and they are often unwilling or unable to suggest practical solutions for new problems. They prefer to avoid public controversy. Many of them went into the sciences because there they found problems that could be dealt with through the application of appropriate techniques providing a kind of certainty.

Journalists, on the other hand, are more interested in policy consequences. They are also more concerned with the "entertainment" role of journalism, which after all, does have to capture audiences. They thrive on controversy and conflict. When all of this is said, we strongly suspect that still another significant reason for journalists' behavior is related to their particular beliefs. A number of studies, have demonstrated the mainstream liberalism of elite journalists, and their tendency to turn for information to public interest groups and "non-establishment" scientists. For journalists, political liberalism has gone hand-in-hand with support for environmental causes. In short, many journalists have taken their cues from environmentalists because they have found the views of such activists congenial on a variety of social issues. John Stossel, who reported the ABC News documentary "Are We Scaring Ourselves to Death?" explained his reasons for believing environmental groups: "We consumer reporters approached it from the bias that on the one hand is business which is greedy and has an ulterior motive and will distort the data, and on the other hand is the noble environmental group, which has no other motive than to help the public" (quoted by Shaw in the *Los Angeles Times*, September 11, 1994, part a, p. 32.).

This is not to suggest that journalists are any more biased than anyone else including academics. Most of them, we dare say, are committed to professional norms of objectivity, fairness and accuracy. They are also committed to publishing "good stories" however much these may contradict their own beliefs. However as Clifford Geertz and others have pointed out, we all tend to see reality in terms of maps which we necessarily create to guide us in the blooming confusion which is the world. As many scholars of the media have pointed out, journalists bring to their work a worldview, which, despite their best intentions, can affect the way they interpret and report. Many events are sufficiently structured so that reporters can and do monitor themselves and describe the events with reasonable accuracy. However, more ambiguous combinations of complicated events inevitably, over time, yield some slippage. Our data show that journalists seeking information about environmental issues tend to turn either to activist government agencies (such as the Environmental Protection Agency) or to various environmental groups as their spokespersons.

These statements may seem strange to some, at least in part because those in the academic community who write about journalists and journalism are more likely to see their reporting as conservative than as liberal. Sometimes reporters are characterized as conservative by these commentators. More often, however, the conservatism of the media is considered to be a function of the influence of editors and publishers (the latter, after all, are businessmen) who are conservative and limit what can be written. Indeed, many academic critics would argue that as the number of newspapers and independent television outlets decline and as various media outlets are increasingly controlled by giant business conglomerates, so reporting inevitably reflects a centrist or right-of-center orientation.

The evidence points in the opposite direction, for not only are reporters liberal but so are many owners of important newspapers, or television networks or media conglomerates themselves liberal, but even when they are not, they feel it incumbent upon themselves to allow their reporters relatively free reign. Indeed, a number of studies have demonstrated that most journalists feel that they are relatively free to determine how they will cover stories with which they are involved. The public is aware of this. While their views are far from unanimous, a significant portion of the newspaper and television audience is persuaded that newspaper and television news does describe reality from a particular perspective. Of those who adhere to this view, a majority believes that the media perspective is liberal. Even liberal respondents are of this opinion. In such matters, of course, liberalism is a matter of perspective. Since the sociologists and political scientists working in the media field tend to be to the left of most journalists in key areas, they naturally regard journalists as taking a conservative perspective. Journalists, on the other hand, while, by and large, persuaded of their objectivity, find radical critiques of their supposed bias more persuasive than they do conservative critiques. This is because they are more likely to identify with academics who are to the left of them than they are to defer to those whom they perceive as being conservative.

The problem is not only that the news *per se* differs from expert opinion, leaving the public poorly informed about cancer risk. The deeper problem is that the public is being misinformed about the nature of expert opinion on cancer risk. The latter is not only a more serious impediment to an informed public, it is a more direct indictment of the journalistic profession. We may not know how to achieve objectivity. We can at least demand accuracy.

Science and Ideology

What can we conclude? It is clear that environmental groups were, for many years (and still are), able to capture the interest and support of the media for claims about the views of scientists which are simply inaccurate. There were many reasons for this, but the end result that bad science has out-pointed good science for some time because ideology has triumphed over evidence. It should be added that while a few scientists have lent their names to bad science, the great majority has not. That, to some, they appear to have done so is partly a reflection of the weakness of media coverage.

It is our experience, though we can only offer anecdotal evidence, that reporting on scientific issues has somewhat improved since we completed our study. Journalists seem to turn now with greater frequency to high quality scientific journals for their information, and are somewhat more skeptical of the claims of environmental groups.

The environmental movement in its early stage was clearly even more ideological than it is now. As it has become part of the establishment and as its composition has changed, it has become more subject to criticism. After all, as Gregg Easterbrook points out, the mainstream movement has won many of its battles, with results that can be easily seen. Beyond that, knowledge about cancer causation and its relation to public policy has been growing among journalists, partly stimulated by the environmental movement itself. The presence of an increasing number of scientifically trained environmentalists has also affected journalists, who have acquired more expertise themselves. For example the Center for Risk Analysis at the Harvard School of Public Health has become an important source of expert information for journalists, as have such environmentally moderate activist groups as the American Council for Science and Health.

Finally, practicing scientists have begun to take a more active role in publicly assessing risks from various activities or substances. The 1995 report by the American Physical Society on the supposed relations between power lines and cancer is a good example of this development. Even so both the media and the public continue to respond to charges that a given man made substance is a carcinogen with what has become known as the "precautionary principle, " i.e., that unless even a useful substance can meet extraordinarily high proof of safety standards, it should be banned. It is also true that the media and, consequently, the public still go into a panic without seriously thinking about the kind of evidence adduced.

Clearly science is a rather fragile endeavor, despite its successes. Human beings do not naturally think scientifically. The point is very well made by Phillip Gerrans who is worth quoting at some length: "Humans are very bad at employing the norms of rationality such as logical inference, probabilistic reasoning and planning beyond the immediate future...even those arenas of human culture consecrated to the norms of rationality."

It is not clear that the American public knows very much about even elementary scientific facts and concepts. A 1996 National Science Foundation study of a cross section of Americans shows that only nine percent of adult Americans know what a molecule is, and only 5 percent can give an explanation of acid rain. More startlingly, less than 50 percent know that the earth orbits the sun annually. It is little wonder, then, that the struggle against the bending of science to serve ideal or material interests never ends.

8

Judicial Fictions: The Supreme Court's Quest for Good Science

Sheila Jasanoff

"Although cross-examination of expert witnesses with the intention of diminishing their credibility is a standard part of the adversarial process, a court appointed scientist, whose character and qualifications have already been established through the nomination-and-selection process, should not be subjected to this type of attack." Barbara S. Hulka, Nancy L. Kerkvliet, and Peter Tugwell, "Experiences of a Scientific Panel Formed to Advise the Federal Judiciary on Silicone Breast Implants."
—*New England Journal of Medicine* 342:812 (2000).

"On the basis of our experience as members of the National Science Panel for the breast-implant litigation, we have made recommendations for the use of similar panels in the future. We believe that such panels should be used more frequently, because they can bring unbiased information about complex scientific and medical issues into the courtroom."

—*Id.,* 815.

Over the last decade or so, the perception has grown in some quarters of the American scientific and legal establishments that the legal system misuses science. The problem, many believe, stems from the inability of lay juries to distinguish between valid scientific claims and "junk science"—expert assertions that would not pass muster with genuine scientists, but that seem nevertheless to carry weight when admitted as testimony before untutored fact-finders. Cross-examination only exacerbates the problem by indiscriminately attacking experts' credibility, whether or not their testimony is technically meritorious. This is a troublesome state of affairs in a society whose courts derive legitimacy as much from seeking the truth as from delivering justice. The standing of the adjudicatory process is gravely compromised if it promiscuously accepts all scientific claims as equally trustworthy, or, worse, if it rejects valid claims on frivolous grounds. If the critics are right, then Barbara Hulka, Nancy

Kerkvliet, and Peter Tugwell, court-appointed experts in the federal silicone gel breast implant litigation, may have a basis for their provocative demand that scientists like them should be exempted from cross-examination, the law's time-tested instrument for uncovering the truth.

To evaluate both the charge and the proposed remedy, we first need to clarify some basic issues about the nature and uses of scientific evidence. How do claims generated for the purpose of resolving legal controversies differ from those arrived at in laboratories and other research settings? Are legal practices more or less effective than scientific ones in revealing error or bias in expert testimony? Should law and science adopt similar standards for the resolution of uncertainty and expert disagreements? And what may the answers to these questions imply for recent efforts to make judges more responsible for the quality of the science presented in their courtrooms?

That questions like these have risen to the forefront of scholarly inquiry is itself a notable phenomenon. The probity of party-selected expert witnesses has long been a concern of legal commentators, but few doubted until the final decades of the twentieth century that the adversary process, with its techniques of discovery and cross-examination, was fundamentally equal to the task of sifting good evidence from bad. The parties' interests, it was assumed, would adequately ensure the integrity of fact-finding, whether the facts in question were mundane or esoteric. The courtroom would simply function as the forum in which the adversaries, each motivated by the desire to win, would vigorously represent their own claims and as diligently contest their opponents'. From this spirited exchange the facts would emerge—or as much of them as needed to resolve disputes fairly. Liberal discovery rules that leveled the playing field for all litigants reflected a basic faith in the efficacy of the adversarial approach. The hope was that the truth would prevail so long as neither side enjoyed an unfair advantage over the other.

Who Shall Judge the Experts?

Only recently has pressure arisen to abandon these classical presumptions in a growing volume of cases involving scientific and technical evidence. Not only the honesty of individual experts, but the whole edifice of adversarial fact-finding is suddenly under attack. In place of a clash of sharply opposed viewpoints, many are now calling for an insulated space in which an expert consensus can be forged away from the rough and tumble of the adversary process. In place of allowing alternative scientific explanations to unfold before a jury, the new vision asks for technical evidence to be developed out of reach of lay skepticism and adversarial confrontation, in judicially managed pretrial proceedings. And in place of the gamesmanship that has traditionally driven the choice of party experts, respected scientific and legal organizations are offering to construct lists of carefully screened experts who will provide courts nothing but the most impartial scientific judgments.

Are these responses warranted? There is good reason to worry about a system of dispute resolution that reduces fact-finding to clashes between hired guns holding extreme positions on opposite sides of an issue. In an age of complex and uncertain relations between science, technology, and society, the notion of arriving at either truth or justice through such bipolar collisions seems curiously antiquated. Yet, as I have argued in earlier writing, courts in the United States have played—and continue to play—a crucial role in the democratization of science and technology. They have accomplished this precisely by not unduly deferring to claims of expertise. Adversarial questioning of experts in legal proceedings has frequently exposed hidden interests and tacit normative assumptions that are embedded in supposedly value-neutral facts. The confrontation of lay and expert viewpoints that the law affords has emerged as a powerful instrument for probing some of the untested epistemological foundations of expert claims.

At its best, the adversary system promotes a more realistic assessment of what experts know, what they legitimately guess at, and what they assert without justification. It makes the *processes* of discovery and invention more transparent and accountable, thereby fostering civic education and social learning. That Americans on the whole seem more optimistic about technology and more trusting of governmental regulation than citizens of other industrial societies arguably has to do with Americans' easier access to the courts when they are injured by technology. Reforms that fundamentally reconfigure the character of legal fact-finding therefore should be held to a fairly high standard of justification. Can we be assured that the move toward judge-driven, in place of party-driven, production of scientific evidence will meet such a standard? Or will another set whose consequences remain as yet safely out of our reckoning simply supplant the perversities of the present system?

The present ferment over scientific evidence and expert witnessing owes much to three important decisions by the U.S. Supreme Court, which, in the 1990s, altered the dynamics of the adversary process by insisting that judges should play a more proactive role in assessing the reliability of expert testimony. I begin with a brief review of these rulings, followed by a critical appraisal of the Court's assumptions about the nature of both scientific and judicial inquiry. I then consider the implications of these judgments in controversies involving substantial scientific uncertainty and conclude that, at least in these cases, they opened the door to unforeseen forms of arbitrariness. My final remarks turn to the perennial problem of balancing of truth and justice in technically complex litigation.

Daubert and Its Progeny

The admissibility of expert evidence rose to the top of the federal judicial agenda in the early 1990s. The Supreme Court, which had never before spoken on the subject, ruled on it three times in quick succession: in *Daubert v. Merrell Dow Pharmaceuticals, Inc.* in 1993; *General Electric Co. v. Joiner* in 1997; and *Kumho Tire Co. v. Carmichael* in 1999. Together, these decisions sought to transform the federal judiciary's traditionally passive posture with respect to expert testimony. Their object was not so much to confer any startlingly new powers on federal judges, who already were authorized to screen offers of expertise under the Federal Rules of Evidence, but rather to challenge the entrenched culture of judicial practice with respect to science. A professional community with only modest claims to scientific competence was urged to insert itself energetically into the assessment of scientific claims. Judges who historically had shied away from usurping the jury's fact-finding role were instructed to exclude inappropriate testimony before it got to trial.

Daubert, the first and most influential of the three cases, grew out of a product liability lawsuit alleging that the anti-nausea drug Bendectin prescribed to women during pregnancy had caused birth defects in their children. The plaintiffs' scientific argument rested largely on data from animal studies and on a controversial, and unpublished, statistical meta-analysis of epidemiological data. The same studies, when disaggregated and reviewed individually, established no significant connection between Bendectin and birth defects. In lawsuits across the country, Bendectin manufacturers won virtually all the cases tried before judges, but juries tended to be significantly more sympathetic toward plaintiffs. In an effort to block future cases from consideration by juries, the defendant drug company urged the Supreme Court in *Daubert* to rewrite the seventy-year-old rule governing the admissibility of scientific evidence in federal courts. Derived from the 1923 decision in *Frye v. United States*, this rule posited that novel scientific evidence should be admitted only if it was generally accepted by the relevant scientific community. The *Daubert* defendant demanded instead that only peer-reviewed, hence published, scientific studies should be deemed admissible.

Writing for the majority, the late Justice Harry Blackmun concluded that admissibility in federal litigation was governed by the congressionally enacted Federal Rules of Evidence and not by the earlier common-law *Frye* rule. Under the legislated rules, judges were authorized to keep out of court any expert testimony that was not both reliable and relevant. The Court encouraged judges to take this mandate seriously, but cautioned that there were no hard-and-fast rules for assessing the reliability of expert opinions. The judge's objective in all cases should be to hold scientific evidence to the kinds of standards that scientists themselves would apply under the circumstances. To further this goal, *Daubert* offered four sample criteria for determining admissibility: was the science in question testable and had it been tested; was it peer reviewed; did it have a known or potential error rate; and, recapitulating *Frye*, was it generally accepted within the relevant scientific community? Many commentators construed *Daubert* as a victory for science because it enjoined federal judges to "think like scientists" in evaluating scientific evidence. In effect, the decision gave rise to a new social persona—that of the trial judge as a gatekeeper for science. A point that drew less notice was that this prescription left judges considerable latitude to decide, in practice, how scientists think.

In *Joiner*, the second of the Supreme Court's rulings on evidence, the plaintiff, a smoker with a family history of cancer, claimed that he had contracted small cell lung cancer as a result of chemical exposure to PCBs. Scientific support for his claim derived from animal studies and from a small number of epidemiological studies whose results had been pooled in accordance with a novel "weight of the evidence methodology." The trial court relied on *Daubert* to exclude all of the plaintiff's testimony as irrelevant or unreliable, thus depriving his case of evidentiary foundation. Effectively, the decision amounted to a dismissal of the plaintiff's claim. The Court of Appeals for the Eleventh Circuit reversed, saying that under the Federal Rules a trial judge's exclusion of expert evidence deserves special scrutiny if, as in this instance, the decision proves to be "outcome determinative." But the Supreme Court flatly rejected this conclusion, holding that there is only one appropriate standard for reviewing *any* evidentiary ruling, regardless of its impact on outcomes. That standard is abuse of discretion—a strict test that was not satisfied in *Joiner* and whose inconsistent application could lead to conflict within and between circuits in post-*Daubert* cases.

For all practical purposes, *Joiner* left trial judges with the last word on most issues of scientific admissibility. But was this a desirable resting place? At least one member of the Court was not convinced. Justice Stephen Breyer, a distinguished administrative lawyer and well-known advocate of expert policymaking, worried that judges lacked the training to make informed discriminations between good and bad science. Breyer therefore proposed a new alliance between courts and working scientists, mediated by authoritative scientific organizations such as the National Academy of Sciences (NAS) and the American Association for the Advancement of Science (AAAS). Bodies like these, he suggested, could provide courts with the names of relevant experts on request. With the scientific community lined up as an ally, trial courts would confidently be able to call upon experts for impartial advice. Judges would no longer need to rely on their own unaided intuitions when confronted by complex and uncertain claims at the frontiers of scientific knowledge.

Justice Breyer's invitation to the scientific community fell on willing ears. One leading scientific organization, the AAAS, soon initiated a demonstration project to establish that the proposed law-science partnership would be feasible in practice. The National Academy of Sciences, for its part, formed a panel on law, science and technology to consider, among other things, how that august body could help the courts to deal with scientific evidence. The Duke Law School's Private Adjudication Center established a register of academic scientists, mostly medical professors, who were willing to serve as court-appointed experts and who, in some cases, were soon called upon to do just that. Developments such as these indicate that Breyer's remarks in *Joiner* created a market for certified "independent" experts who would provide their services directly to the courts, and that scientific as well as legal institutions quickly geared up to meet the increased demand.

In *Kumho*, the last of the big evidence decisions, the Supreme Court's attention shifted from science, narrowly defined, to the wider issue of technical expertise in general. The plaintiffs in this case had been driving a minivan whose right rear tire blew out; the resulting accident killed one passenger and severely injured others. The plaintiffs charged that the blowout was caused by a defect in the design or manufacture of the minivan's steel-belted radial tire. To support their contention, they presented testimony by Dennis Carlson, Jr., an engineer and expert in tire failure analysis, who offered his informed opinion that the blowout occurred not through misuse or ordinary wear but because of a defect in the tire. The district court mechanically applied the four *Daubert* criteria to Carlson's evidence, found that it failed these tests, and hence deemed it inadmissible. The Court of Appeals for the Eleventh Circuit reversed on the ground that *Daubert* applied only to scientific evidence and not to technical matters such as the analysis of tire treads or tread marks. Again, the Supreme Court disagreed, holding that *Daubert*'s gatekeeping mandate extends not only to science but also to non-scientific expert evidence, such as engineering, which should be held to similar levels of "intellectual rigor." Writing for the majority, however, Justice Breyer cautioned that the *Daubert* criteria were meant to be regarded as helpful, not definitive, and hence should not be indiscriminately applied to all decisions concerning the admissibility of technical evidence.

Judging Science: Myths and Realities

The U.S. legal system takes for granted that judges should not behave like legislators, let alone like political scientists or sociologists of science. The moral authority of the courts depends in no small part on tending the boundary between law and policy and confining judges' activities demonstrably to the side of the law. There, judicial discretion is constrained by the relative impartiality of the constitution, legislation, prior decisions, and well-understood rules of reasoning; on the policy side, by contrast, lies a messy world of trade-offs and choices, whose resolution makes judging come perilously close to politics by other means.

Judges, especially appellate judges, are conscious too that their command of abstract legal principles far exceeds their in-depth, practical experience of how the world works, even within the relatively confined world of law enforcement. Indeed, federal courts have incurred the most vehement criticism when they have strayed over the perceived line between law and policy, as for instance in historic decisions over school busing, which disrupted the operation of urban school districts around the country, or the so-called Miranda warnings, named after the 1966 decision in *Miranda v. Arizona*, which encroached upon well-established routines of police practice. (Controversial in its time, *Miranda* was recently upheld by the Supreme Court because the justices recognized that the case had actually succeeded in altering police behavior in the intervening decades.) To avoid such controversies, courts seek not only to argue tightly from precedent, but also, as far as possible, to eschew generic prescriptions in favor of rulings limited to the particularities of cases. Thus, even in *Daubert*, where there was unanimity on the narrow legal principle that the Federal Rules of Evidence had supplanted *Frye*, Chief Justice Rehnquist dissented in part, saying that the Court had strayed beyond its competence in proposing general standards by which the lower courts should evaluate scientific evidence. Such standards, he argued, should emerge case by case, deriving meaning and authority from the specific factual circumstances they were designed to address.

Did *Daubert*'s seemingly innocuous injunction that trial judges should screen evidence in accordance with scientists' standards represent, in practice, an ill-considered foray into judicial policymaking? To explore this question, let us examine three assumptions that the triad of evidence decisions made about the nature of science and the capacity of courts. First, the *Daubert* majority seemed to believe that the criteria of scientific validity would be clear and exogenously given, even in litigation contexts. Judges accordingly would be able to apply them to the evidence, consistently, objectively, and without abuse of discretion, as required by *Joiner*. Second, the Court was persuaded that "thinking like scientists" would enable judges to review scientific and technical evidence without prejudicial bias. *Scientists*, on this view, were assumed to be free from systematic biases that might distort the outcomes of legal decision-making. Third, the Court presumed that judges would be able to carry out their screening function without detracting from the jury's constitutionally mandated role.

As we shall see, all three assumptions are open to question. The reality that judges confront when dealing with scientific evidence is considerably more murky than the Supreme Court envisaged. In rejecting as flawed one approach to fact-finding—that of the adversary process—the Court opted for another without fully evaluating its social and political, let alone its epistemological, implications. Consequently, admissibility rulings in the post-*Daubert* era have opened up new possibilities for arbitrary action, as judges either hold science to *ad hoc* tests of reliability or else uncritically incorporate into their rulings the biases of dominant expert communities.

The Validity of "Litigation Science"

The concept of judicial gatekeeping with respect to scientific evidence makes most sense if the evidence offered by the parties can be evaluated in accordance with well-articulated, externally determined criteria of validity on which there is, ideally, a high degree of consensus. Only then may courts reasonably look to the scientific community for guidance on the applicable standards. That the principles for determining validity are in fact rather more elusive than the high court imagined became clear as soon as *Daubert* was remanded for reconsideration to the Ninth Circuit Court of Appeals. In its earlier ruling, the Ninth Circuit had upheld the trial court's decision, on the basis of *Frye*, to exclude the scientific testimony offered by the plaintiffs. Now that *Frye* no longer applied, a three-judge panel headed by Judge Alex Kosinski had to decide whether the plaintiffs' evidence met the new admissibility standard set forth by the Supreme Court.

Acknowledging its "heady task" and taking "a deep breath," the appellate court quickly concluded that *Daubert*'s four sample criteria were not sufficient. Nothing daunted, the court created an additional test relating the credibility of the proffered testimony to the timing of the research underlying it. The significant issue, the court observed in what we will call *Daubert II*, was whether the experts were proposing to testify about "matters growing naturally and directly out of research they have conducted independent of the litigation, or whether they [had] developed their opinions expressly for purposes of testifying" (*Daubert v. Merrell Dow Pharmaceuticals, Inc.*, 43 F.3d 1311 (9th Cir. 1995), p. 317). If the research predated the litigation, the court concluded, there is "important, objective proof that the research comports with the dictates of good science." In the Bendectin case, none of the plaintiffs' experts had engaged in pre-litigation research; nor had they published their results in peer-reviewed journals, thus falling short of one of *Daubert*'s explicit criteria. On this basis, the Ninth Circuit excluded the plaintiff's testimony and dismissed the case.

In comparing the reliability of pre- and post-litigation science, the *Daubert II* judges acted, in effect, as amateur sociologists of science, pronouncing on how the validity of scientific findings relates to the practice of scientists. Not surprisingly, they found themselves on shaky empirical ground. To begin with, in many recent lawsuits, most if not all of the evidence presented by the parties on either side has rested on research undertaken after the initiation of the action. Lack of definitive knowledge can itself be a powerful driver of litigation. For example, little or nothing was known about the possible health effects of silicone gel breast implants when individual claims of disease and injury from these devices snowballed into a huge class action involving some 450, 000 claimants. In this case as in many others, it was the legal conflict that helped to crystallize the scientific issues—to make them intellectually tractable, economically significant, and deserving of the scientific community's attention and effort. Ongoing research, moreover, closed some issues but opened others. The Ninth Circuit's test would treat all the evidence generated in episodes of this kind as equally suspect, although there is every reason to believe that post-litigation science spans the same spectrum from reliable to unreliable as pre-litigation science. Timing alone is hardly a compelling indicator of quality. The key determinants, regardless of the timing of research, have to do with the methods and processes that scientists adopt to ensure the validity of their findings.

The assumption that pre-litigation science is necessarily more objective than science produced for litigation rests, as well, on an insupportably idealized notion of "pure" science as a disinterested field of inquiry. In an era of increasing cooperation between universities and industry, as well as biomedical researchers' growing financial stakes in the fruits of their labor, the positing of such a sphere of objective inquiry seems highly problematic. Besides, studies of laboratory science have consistently displayed, even in the secluded ivory tower, a far from dispassionate world, in which competition is intense, corners are cut, and claims are frequently rushed into print without satisfying conventional tests of objectivity. Again, it appears that validity should not be regarded as an automatic attribute of research conducted independently of litigation. Regardless of the context in which research is done, concrete steps must be taken to shore up its reliability. It is the nature of this validating work that should be the focus of the fact-finders' inquiry.

The Biases of Science

How impartial, in any event, are the critical faculties that scientists bring to the evaluation of each other's claims? Are the internal review mechanisms of science as effective in exposing bias as the techniques of questioning experts in court? Unlike scientific peer review, whose object often is to improve or clarify the presentation of data, cross-examination (as the members of the silicone gel expert panel implicitly recognized) is an intrinsically unfriendly procedure. It seeks to discredit the testimony and, if need be, its presenter. The experienced cross-examiner strategically blurs the distinctions between personal and professional credibility, recognizing that contradictions in sworn or published statements and revealed financial ties to the defendant may fatally damage an expert's authority. Jurors with relatively little appreciation of science may be at a loss to discriminate between serious methodological deficiencies and superficial contradictions revealed through cross-examination. For these reasons, scientists often regard cross-examination as a manipulative, even abusive instrument, ill-suited to eliciting the truth.

At the same time, precisely because it is a hostile technique, cross-examination of expert witnesses may reveal biases and assumptions that went unnoticed by members of their own peer communities. Thus, the notorious O.J. Simpson murder trial, in which the jury was roundly criticized for its disregard of DNA evidence, underscored a previously under-emphasized weak link in the production of such data. The defense's skilful cross-examination of the criminalist Denis Fung established many points at which the collection of samples could have been mishandled or tampered with. This demonstration prompted police departments thereafter to pay much more attention to the standardization of crime-scene behavior.

It is interesting to compare this result with that in *People v. Castro*, the 1989 case that helped to disclose numerous messy practices and questionable methodological assumptions adopted by private DNA testing companies. In *Castro*, an unplanned and unprecedented meeting between prosecution and defense experts led to the spotlighting of deficiencies in claims about the reliability of DNA evidence. Previously, emphasis on the power and precision of molecular biology had seduced the majority of the scientific community, and initially also the courts, into unquestioning acceptance of the new technique. No one had looked too closely at the error-prone human practices through which invisible bits of DNA are converted into readable "matches" that almost uniquely identify the perpetrator. *Castro*, accordingly, has been seen as providing support for wider use of court-appointed expert panels who can think outside the constraining polarities of the adversary process. Yet, the case also indicates that such bodies may be more effective at spotting issues *within* the conventional framing of scientific and technical controversies than they are at questioning the boundaries of "science" itself.

Scientific inquiry achieves its precision and power by explicitly circumscribing the boundaries within which it is carried out. These boundaries may be defined in part by a governing research tradition, which the philosopher Thomas Kuhn called a paradigm. Equally, however, science bounds itself off by various means from collateral social practices—politics, religion, faith healing—whose purposes and methods might dilute the institutional authority of science. These bounding strategies are ordinarily highly effective. Neither a working biologist nor the proverbial man on the street, for example, would think to label the activities of a crime-scene specialist as a part of "DNA science." Yet, the rhetoric of DNA-typing's infallibility begins to have meaning only after a sample is removed from its mundane and messy point of origin and safely deposited in a testing laboratory, where it can undergo precise, scientifically validated manipulation; even then, as *Castro* revealed, the technique's reliability may be compromised by inevitable errors in testing. The criminalist's activities, then, are just as indispensable as lab tests to the production of the "fingerprint" that ultimately convicts or exonerates a criminal. The integrity of the evidence depends on the entire process being above reproach, from sample collection to the eventual interpretation and courtroom representation of data. As long as courts took for granted the boundaries of DNA science laid down by experts on testing, they also accepted without question the claims of near-perfect accuracy made on behalf of the technology. Only after successive lawsuits breached several tacit boundaries—between "science" and crime-scene methods, between *making* and *interpreting* autoradiographs, and between molecular biology and less certain methods in biostatistics—were significant questions raised about the reliability of expert testimony about DNA.

The recommendation to "think like scientists" presumes as well that scientists will behave no differently when advising the courts about legal evidence from the way they do when evaluating claims within their own expert communities. In courtroom contexts, however, scientists not infrequently offer opinions that extend beyond their specific areas of competence. Ordinary judicial vigilance, boosted perhaps by post-*Daubert* self-confidence, has sufficed in the past to prevent the most common forms of overreaching, as when courts have kept physicians from testifying on the condition of patients whom they never examined. But courts may find themselves substantially more vulnerable to newer forms of scientific advice-giving encouraged by the Supreme Court's evidence rulings. For, in an unlooked-for symmetry, *Daubert* has prompted scientists to think like judges as much as it encouraged judges to play the part of scientists. In law review articles and briefs to the courts, scientists have put forward additional tests of validity to supplement those offered in *Daubert*. They have also suggested significant rule changes in the trial of tort claims: for example, that showings of general causation should always take precedence over specific causation or that epidemiological evidence should always be weighted more than animal studies. These sorts of prescriptions instruct the legal process, in effect, on how to deal with uncertainty, although doing justice in modern societies may demand that the law's aims and methods for coping with uncertainty should *not* be the same as those of science.

In science, uncertainty is simply a measure of the probability that a given observation or explanation may not in fact be correct. Uncertainty may be reduced by defining a phenomenon more exactly, generating more data, ruling out alternate causes, persuading dissenters, or formulating new causal models. All of these steps may take more time than is available, as a practical matter, within the institutional constraints of litigation. Moreover, the methods by which science reduces uncertainty in pristine laboratory conditions—by painstakingly eliminating all possible confounding factors—may be impossible to achieve in the complex, real-world situations that give rise to contemporary legal claims. Do silicone gel breast implants cause atypical connective tissue disease? Can an ecosystem damaged by oil spills recover its full vitality? Was it pilot error, defective maintenance, or a poorly designed part that caused the airplane crash? New methods of measuring, monitoring, and interpreting health, safety or environmental effects may need to be devised to address such questions, and these will invariably prove controversial. In practice, then, uncertainty in the litigation context can sometimes be bounded but often not completely reduced.

Uncertainty about scientific findings does not have to disqualify them for use in evidence. It affects the weight of evidence, which juries are competent to consider, rather than its admissibility, which is a matter for judges. Determining admissibility, however, is one point in the legal process at which courts can decide where to place the burden of pragmatically irreducible uncertainty. A favored approach through much of the twentieth century was to lower the burden of proof for plaintiffs in cases where current science was incapable of producing definitive evidence. Such moves necessarily widened the distance between scientific proof and legal proof, but they effectuated the courts' institutional mandate to decide how much of the cost of what we do not know should fall on injured and unsuspecting victims.

None of this implies that the law should be indifferent with respect to the validity of expert testimony. It does mean that the law may appropriately settle for something less than scientifically accepted truth in order to further the interests of justice. In practical terms, *Daubert* does not preclude the admissibility of studies that are still provisional—that have not, for instance, undergone scrutiny over a period of years or been formally replicated. Needless to say, studies that have been validated in these ways (for example, studies of cancer caused by asbestos or tobacco) may legitimately command greater respect in legal settings than those that have not (for example, studies of birth defects related to Bendectin). But such judgments of relative credibility rest on criteria that are in no sense esoteric and, if cogently presented, should be well within the competence of average jurors.

Judges as Juries

How valid, finally, is the Supreme Court's assumption that judges themselves will not usurp the jury's function by playing a more proactive role in the assessment of evidence? It is worth recalling that there are several reasons why federal judges historically refrained from aggressive use of pretrial screening and court-appointed experts, even after these practices were officially sanctioned by the Federal Rules of Evidence. One, which the emerging institutional alliances between science and law are seeking to correct, is the courts' lack of knowledge about how to locate the appropriate expertise. But other factors also promote self-restraint, chief among them the courts' commitment to the transparency of the adversary process and to jury deliberations as the constitutionally mandated instrument for fact-finding. Improved access to experts will not address these latter concerns. Judges, for instance, may bring to the evaluation of evidence experiential biases that will pass unchallenged in the absence of hostile cross-examination. Thus, in an Oregon trial involving breast implants, the plaintiffs argued that the presiding judge, Robert Jones, could not neutrally screen the evidence because his wife had been fitted with implants following cancer surgery. The judge declined to recuse himself on these grounds, claiming that his wife's experience would not color his ability to ensure that the evidence comported with state-of-the-art science. In the post-*Joiner* era, his would be the last word on the subject.

Even when federal judges have no prior views on the subject matter of individual cases, they cannot be expected to approach their task with minds empty of preconceived notions about science. As members of a highly educated professional elite in an industrial society, they necessarily bring to the bench a variety of understandings, nurtured since early childhood, about the nature of facts, rationality, progress, and the scientific method. These background beliefs provide a ready resource for judges to draw on when confronted by the contingencies of particular cases, especially when (as Judge Kosinski found in *Daubert II*) the *Daubert* criteria fail to provide adequate guidance. On the whole, judicial instincts in such matters can be expected to converge with those of scientists, with whom they share important elements of social and educational formation. Judges accordingly may be less likely than culturally heterogeneous juries to question the standards and boundaries set by scientists. The differences between the judge-tried and jury-tried Bendectin cases can be interpreted as reflecting just such a divergence of underlying world views, rather than the juries' failure to understand or properly credit the scientific evidence.

There seems little question, then, that active judicial gatekeeping will produce pockets of scientific claims-making that are not accessible to cross-checking by plaintiffs in the same way as testimony offered in open court under the traditional rules of adversary litigation. Insights from the sociology of science back up the general sociological expectation that judicial alliances with mainstream science will reinforce the scientific status quo and raise the entry barriers against speculative, unpublished, or controversial claims. One may well wonder whether the *Daubert* majority, led by the liberal Justice Blackmun and beating back the defendants' plea to admit only peer-reviewed science into evidence, intended to bring about such a sea change in the resolution of complex and technically uncertain claims.

Two Views of Science

The public debate about the role and powers of court-appointed experts shows itself, in the light of this discussion, as the substitute for a deeper, sociologically more interesting question. Whose representation of how science works should drive changes in the process of legal fact-finding? The view that tacitly animated the high court's opinions in *Daubert* and its progeny is shared by the majority of working scientists. According to this perception, there is nothing inherently problematic about distinguishing between mainstream and marginal scientific evidence. It is merely a matter of finding and applying the appropriate criteria. If courts lack the necessary expertise, they can turn to science itself for three kinds of assistance: first, for rosters of experts to provide relevant and reliable information and analysis; second, for help in contextualizing or making sense of difficult technical arguments; and third, for criteria with which to discriminate between legitimate science and mere snake oil. All that judges have to do, in this reading of the situation, is to reach out and accept the wisdom of the responsible scientific community. Juries, in many cases, need not enter the picture at all, since the court-science partnership should rule out most frivolous claims at the threshold. At the extreme, this vision would substitute for the common law's unruly, adversarial development of facts something akin to European civil law's disciplined, magisterial approach to fact-finding. This is the position that Hulka, Kerkvliet, and Tugwell advocated on the basis of their experience in the breast implant litigation.

A sharply contrasting view has emerged from the sociology of science and law, and it is significantly less complacent. Empirical research in these fields indicates that the "science" needed to resolve legal conflicts is seldom ready to hand when the action begins. Not only do lawsuits increasingly depend for their resolution on "post-litigation science, " in Judge Kosinski's sense of the term, but the very genesis of these conflicts reflects, in part, the absence of pre-existing, scientifically validated, causal stories relevant to the plaintiffs' troubles. Evidentiary science is therefore produced in a field already configured by the parties' interests and assumptions. Moreover, the novelty of the issues ensures that—to a considerable degree—even the standards of what counts as good science have to be determined under the contingent and contested circumstances of individual cases. Under these conditions, it is difficult to imagine any evidence that simply and without bias represents a "mainstream" scientific view. In the highly contingent environment of litigation, it is virtually unthinkable that either judges or their appointed experts could embrace any scientific explanation in a neutral manner: as the quotations from the silicone gel panel members suggest, experts are too caught up in constructing the criteria by which their own performance must, in the end, be evaluated.

Implementing *Daubert*, then, requires judges not simply to think like scientists, but to choose between competing accounts of science as it relates to legal decision-making. By unreflectively embarking on this process, judges behave like naïve sociologists of science, accountable neither to the parties nor to scholarly opinion outside the hermetic world of judicial decision-making. The judiciary's background beliefs about science, in turn, shape the process of generating the evidence, and so, inevitably, its content. This is scarcely equivalent to the neutral application of readily available expert tests and standards contemplated by *Daubert* and *Kumho*.

The Burden of Uncertainty

Daubert, *Joiner*, and *Kumho* responded to a particular framing of the problem of law and science: how, in the context of adversarial litigation, can courts most effectively ensure that judgments will not be swayed by "junk science"? The answer in all three opinions was that courts should actively enter into screening the evidence and defer more to scientists. In hindsight, it appears that this framing of the issue may have sidestepped the problem of uncertainty that lies at the heart of much technically complex litigation. Courts were led to focus too narrowly on the truth and reliability of technical claims, when the deeper question for society is how to remedy harms if the facts cannot be definitively established, inside or outside the legal process.

The curious turn in evidence law signaled by *Daubert* has opened up new concerns. The indeterminacy of science when lawsuits begin gives judges unexpected leeway to inject their biases into the construction of relevant facts. And even if the criteria for judging science are relatively clear-cut, as assumed by the majority, a partnership between judges and scientists to pre-screen technical evidence sits uneasily in a constitutional system that entrusts fact-finding to juries. *A priori*, too, there is little basis for crediting lay judges with greater scientific sophistication than possessed by other lay fact-finders. By contrast, there is reason to suspect that an elite judiciary will defer more often to science's institutional authority, with consequent loss of critical capacity in the adjudicatory process.

Questioning *Daubert*'s simple faith in exogenous validation criteria does not have to leave courts without resources for controlling the quality of scientific evidence. Judges, for instance, have used their case management powers effectively to force the parties to delimit more precisely the issues between them. Judicially enforced settlement, still the most common outcome of litigation, permits courts to factor in the uncertainties of the evidence, along with considerations of responsibility and blame. Court-appointed experts and panels can play a positive role by producing context-specific knowledge, although extravagant claims for their neutrality—let alone their right to be shielded from the adversary process—should be treated with extreme skepticism. And in the post-*Daubert* era, judges are more likely to exercise their own critical faculties to ensure that widely accepted standards of reliability are respected in the production of scientific and technical evidence.

The most heroic efforts to get the science right, finally, cannot resolve the problem of what to do when knowledge is uncertain or wholly lacking or how to allocate equitably the burdens of irreducible uncertainty. My own view is that much more creativity is needed on the side of fashioning remedies for injured parties in what the German sociologist Ulrich Beck has labeled the "risk society." Beck refers to the fact that, in contemporary societies, risks have seemingly ramified without corresponding evolution in the structures of management, compensation, and control. America's distaste for comprehensive insurance, for example, has left the deeply conservative institutions of the law with frontline responsibility for striking the balance between technological advances and care for technology's unintended victims. Fortunately, common-law courts have shown great ingenuity in tailoring remedies to fit the facts and contingencies of particular cases. They have done so in the past by uncoupling remedial concerns from a potentially unhelpful search for definitive causes. Instead, the extent and nature of compensation have been crafted to take into account the state of knowledge, as well as the blame, if any, for its gaps and deficiencies. *This* kind of balancing is well within the courts' institutional competence. It leads them not into the unfamiliar, and risky, territory of thinking like scientists, but back to the familiar, if no less arduous, process of reflecting like judges.

References

Angell, Marcia. 1996. *Science on Trial: The Clash of Medical Evidence and the Law in the Breast Implant Case*. New York: Norton.
Beck, Ulrich. 1992. *Risk Society: Towards a New Modernity*. London: Sage.
Foster, Kenneth R. and Peter W. Huber. 1997. *Judging Science: Scientific Knowledge and the Federal Courts*. Cambridge, MA: MIT Press.
Jasanoff, Sheila. 1995. *Science at the Bar: Law, Science, and Technology in America*. Cambridge, MA: Harvard University Press.
Sanders, Joseph. 1998. *Bendectin on Trial: A Study of Mass Tort Litigation*. Ann Arbor: University of Michigan Press.
Smith, Roger and Brian Wynne, eds. 1998. *Expert Evidence: Interpreting Science in the Law*. London: Routledge.

Contributor's List

Joel Best is professor and chair of the Department of Sociology and Criminal Justice at the University of Delaware. His books include *Threatened Children, Random Violence*, and *Damned Lies and Statistics*.

Norval Glenn is Ashbel Smith Professor of Sociology and Stiles Professor of American Studies at the University of Texas at Austin, where he teaches courses on the family and survey research methods. He is also research director of the Council on Families at the Institute for American Values.

Jonathan B. Imber is editor-in-chief of *Society*, and Class of 1949 Professor in Ethics and Professor of Sociology at Wellesley College.

Sheila Jasanoff is professor of science and public policy at Harvard University's John F. Kennedy School of Government and the School of Public Health.

Mark A. R. Kleiman is professor of policy studies at the UCLA School of Public Policy and Social Research. He is the author of *Against Excess: Drug Policy for Results* and *Marijuana: Costs of Abuse, Costs of Control*.

Judith Kleinfeld is professor of psychology and director of the Northern Studies Program at the University of Alaska Fairbanks. She has published extensively on gender issues and her research has been reported in the *New York Times, Wall Street Journal, Atlantic Monthly, Psychology Today, Chronicle of Higher Education, Education Week*, and other periodicals. She has won numerous awards for her research on the education of children with fetal alcohol syndrome and on gender issues.

S. Robert Lichter is director of the Center for Media and Public Affairs at Smith College. He is the co-author (with Stanley Rothman) of *Environmental Cancer: A Political Disease?* (1999).

Robert J. MacCoun is professor of public policy and professor of law at the University of California at Berkeley, and co-author (with Peter Reuter) of the forthcoming *Drug War Heresies: Learning from Other Vices, Times, and Places.*

Allan Mazur, a sociologist and an engineer, is professor of public affairs in the Maxwell School of Syracuse University, and Gilbert White Fellow at Resources for the Future in Washington, DC. He is author most recently of *A Hazardous Inquiry: The Rashomon Effect at Love Canal.*

Stanley Rothman is Mary Huggins Gamble Professor of Government Emeritus at Smith College in Northampton, Massachusetts, and the director of the college's Center for the Study of Social and Political Change. He is the co-author (with S. Robert Lichter) of *Environmental Cancer: A Political Disease?* (1999).

Name Index

Amato, Paul, 73
Ames, Bruce, 90
Anderson, Anne, 40-41
Anderson, Jimmie, 40

Bair, E. Scott, 45
Beck, Ulrich, xiv
Benford, Gregory, 36
Berger, Peter, vii
Best, Joel viii, x
Birgeneau, Robert J., 15, 18-19, 23, 27
Blackmun, Harry, l01, 112
Booth, Alan, 73
Breyer, Stephen, 102-103

Carlson, Dennis, Jr., 103
Cherlin, Andrew, 72-73
Clarke, Harriett, 42-45
Clinton, Bill, 21
Clinton, Hillary, 21
Condlin, Robert, 47
Coulsey, Jean, 44

Doll, Richard, 90
Douglas, Mary, 92

Easterbrook, Gregg, 95
Epstein, Samuel, 90

Fox, Robert, 44

Geertz, Clifford, 93
Gill, Richard, 73
Glenn, Norval, xii
Greenfield, Jeff, 26

Harr, Jonathan 39
Hausman, Patricia, 16-17
Holden, Constance, 23, 28

Hopkins, Nancy, 16, 19, 21-22, 26
Hulka, Barbara, 97, 112

Imber, Jonathan, 28

Jasanoff, Sheila, xiii

Kalven, Harry, 36
Keith, Bruce, 73
Kerkvliet, Nancy 98, 112
Kilpatrick, Jimmy, 25
Kilty, Kevin, 28
Kleiman, Mark, xi, xii
Kleinfeld, Judith, ix
Kleitman, Daniel, 22
Kosinski, Alex, 105, 112
Kuhn, Thomas, 108

Lawler, Andrew, 28
Leo, John, 22
Lichter, S. Robert, xii, xiii

MacCoun, Robert J., x, 34
Madison, James, 20
Matthews, June, 20
Mayer, Susan, 74
Mazur, Allan, xi, xiii
McCaffrey, Barry, 34-35
McLanahan, Sara, 74

Nesson, Charles, 46-47

Pacelle, Mitchell, 43, 45
Paulos, John Allen, 6
Peto, Richard, 90
Pollack, Harold, 53
Potter, Mary C., l9

Recer, Paul, 33, 35

Rehnquist, William, 104
Reuter, Peter, x, 32, 34, 56
Rothman, Stanley, xii, xiii

Schlichtmann, Jan, 46
Shaw, Bernard, 26
Shils, Edward, vii, viii
Skinner, Walter, 42-45
Snyder, Mitch, 6
Sommers, Christina Hoff, 4
Steiger, James H., 16-17

Stossel, John, 93
Sunstein, Cass, 28

Tugwell, Peter, 98, 112

Whithead, Barbara Dafoe, 74
Wildavsky, Aaron, 92
Wilson, Robin, 21, 23
Wolfe, Sidney, 90

Zeisel, Hans, 36